Bitter or Better; it is your choice

Acknowledgments

I want to thank the wonderful, Godly, Spiritual leaders I have had throughout this health journey. God used their messages to speak to my heart. There were times these men were preaching that it seemed time would stop, Heaven would open, and I be told "that was for you"

Gardendale First Baptist in Gardendale Alabama - Dr. Steve Gaines, Mark Harrison, Dr. Kevin Hamm

Calvary Baptist Church in Batesville Mississippi - Dr. Paul Middleton

Mt. Hebron Baptist Church in Spruce Pine Alabama- Jerome Sherill, Gary Yeilding and Scott Delashaw

Bitter or Better; it is your choice

Mercy and Grace

I want to start by telling a story that few people know. All that you are about to read; almost did not happen. Mercy is the deliverance from judgment that we deserve. Grace is the extending of a Blessing to the unworthy.

Both were bestowed upon me at the age of twelve. I was deeply under Spiritual conviction during the Summer of 1973. In church when the invitation was given, I would hold to the bench in front of me. During July my dad took me, my sister and a friend to the creek to swim. I did not know how to swim! The three of us were playing on inner tubes in about waist deep water. I remember my dad was sitting in a lawn chair in the shallow water.

I stepped to get the inner tube, into an unseen deep hole. I managed to get out a yelp as I went under. I reached bottom and pushed upward; I see my dad getting out of the chair. I go back under to the bottom. I push upward and as I break surface, I see my dad about knee deep heading toward me.

Back under I the water I go, I am struggling and tired. I push upward and this time I see dad in chest deep water; pushing to get to me. I go back under. In case you lost count that is three times.

I am swimming in blue jeans and am weighted down to the bottom. With what oxygen I have, I push up with all I have left. As I break the surface of the water; dad grabs me.

He pulls me to the bank where I cough and spit up creek water for a few moments. We go home and as we enter the door, I remember my mom asking, "did you all have fun?" I said yes, "But I almost drown!"

I had my thirteenth birthday on August 6. The next week we had revival at our church. This is the revival where noon service was held, and then we came back that night for more. It would go from Sunday through Friday. I again held the pew tight and made it through another invitation. That night I had a very vivid dream.

I was in my back yard by myself just throwing a ball. Suddenly, the entire word turned into fire. I then heard very evil laughter and I realized I was in Hell. I started screaming and then I woke up. I ran too my parents' room just to make sure the rapture had not occurred. I asked Jesus into my life immediately.

The next night as soon as the invitation was given, I tapped Ron on the shoulder and made it to alter as quickly as possible. I knew I was saved but I had to let everyone know.

I firmly believe those four snap shots of my dad symbolize what Jesus did for me. Dad kept coming to save me even if it meant danger to him. Jesus died on the cross to save me eternally. He gave me one more chance, that fourth time out of the water; to offer me the gift of salvation.

Bitter or Better; it is your choice

My Background

What is the worst thing that has ever happened to you? What are the worst words you have ever been told? Those are some of the things I reflect on when I look back over the years. What was I so involved in that I thought it couldn't get any worse? Trust me, it can and did get worse.

I have been hesitant to write this story. I guess if I write it then the story is finished. However, God has placed on me to write. Therefore, I will write. This is not my story! This is His story and I merely have allowed Him to use me.

As you read this story, I want you to allow yourself to draw close to what God wants you to do and not what you want to do!

After 22 years of marriage, I was told she wanted a divorce. 22 years and children ages 16 and 19, and you want a divorce! After seeing there would be no reconciliation, I was like fine that what you will get. The divorce was completed in January 2003, and I buried my feelings and threw myself into work. As manager I had plenty to do and to plan, so I worked. I did not allow God to help me through the process.

In June of 2004 I had everything going for me, by the world's view. I was a mid-level manager with Alabama Power over the Tuscaloosa office. With 23 employees and a $5 million dollar budget I was busy. I had progressed through various positions and was hopeful of taking the next step up when my supervisor retired. I was busy outside of work also. I had bought 80 acres (about the area of a large shopping mall) of land. I had bought a boat, Sea doo, 4-wheeler. So, I had the trappings of success.

Do you notice ALL the I statement in the above paragraph? It wasn't supposed to be like that. You see when I was thirteen years old, I accepted Jesus Christ as my personal Savior. I gave my life to Him to use and for Him to be my guide. Through High School, four years in the Air Force and completion of college I had Him in front. Somehow though in my career, I had pushed Him to the back.

I fell victim to the busyness of success by my standards, instead of God's standards. I tell people that I do not believe the burning bush was the first time Moses had felt God presence. The Bible states that Moses went farther out into the desert. I always wondered what that could mean. I was about to find out.

People ask sometimes, why does bad things happen to good people? The Bible clearly tells that it rains on the just and the unjust (Matthew 5:45, KJV). Problems hit everyone, the difference with a Believer is we have someone to carry us through the storm.

To understand where I am, I always remember where I came from. I was raised in a community called

Bitter or Better; it is your choice

Wiginton, Alabama, a very rural area. I went to school at Hackleburg whose population was around 1,100 in the 60's and 70's. Looking back our family was poor. The strange thing was we never realized it. We had a house to live in, food on the table, and love.

I watched my mom work in a textile factory that physically wore her out. This was before cushioned floor mats and ergonomic workstations. It was back breaking work done while standing on concrete all day. My dad was a carpenter and worked in construction. By the time I was eight years old he worked out of town. He would leave on Sunday evening and arrive back on Friday evening. My brother, sister and I did the household work and there was no allowance. We were just expected to do the work and we did it.

At Hackleburg high school I played sports, and this is where I learned to never quit. My football coach pushed us to do our best. We only won three games my senior year, but it is one of my prouder moments. Even though we not as talented; we gave it all we had. Coach Gary Smith wouldn't let us quit. This being instilled in me would come back to help me later in life.

It was during high school that I realized I was going to go a different path. I worked one summer with my dad on a construction job in 90-degree heat and knew that it was not for me. I was going to find a way to go to college and be the boss. My mom would always tell me "Be good to those on your way up, because you don't know who you will meet on your way down." This quote became so vital in my health battle that would come.

After graduation I started at Northwest AL Junior College. I took a full load of classes during the day and worked a full 3-11 shift in housekeeping at Lister Hill Hospital. I traveled a triangle five days a week. Home to school (12 miles), school to work (25 miles), and then work to home (15 miles). After a year I had made good grades, but I realized that physically and financially I would never pull it off. This is when I made the decision to join the Air Force.

After basic training and technical training in Texas, I spent the next three and a half years at Mountain Home AFB in Idaho. An Air Force base is its own city. Everything you need is offered. Boise State University held night classes on base. I took advantage of this while saving money to complete my degree when I was discharged in November 1983. I knew that enlisted life was not for me. I just couldn't handle the bureaucracy.

Upon completion of my four years, I moved back home, with wife and a one-year-old daughter. I heard Lee Trevino talk about pressure one time as being on the 18th hole to win a match and the only money you have is the change rattling in your pocket. Well, I understand this very well. I had two years of course work to complete my degree. I had to take and pass each course to be able to take the more advanced class. I also only had money saved for four semesters of college. That is true pressure, there was no dropping a class or a do over, I had to pass every class.

I enrolled at the University of North Alabama in January 1984. I cannot say enough about the professors and leadership at UNA. The school was perfect because you could see a professor if you had a question. There I met the Dean of Business School, Dr. Knight. He is the one that encouraged me to complete a Double Major in Accounting and Management. By taking specific electives instead of general electives; I graduated with my Bachelor of Science degree in May 1985. Along with my double major I also had a minor in Office Administration.

Bitter or Better; it is your choice

Upon graduation I had the next major decision, what would be my career path? As I approached graduation I applied for and was accepted into the Air Force Officer Training School. I had the date set and my first assignment. All I had to do was sign the paperwork. However, God had a different plan.

During Christmas of 1984 a family friend, Cullen Isom, stopped by and encouraged me to apply at Alabama Power. I applied for a management trainee program and forgot about it. During Spring Break in March, I received a call to come in for interview with H.R. in Tuscaloosa. While I was talking to the Manager, Mr. Lamon, he called the Division Accounting Manager, Mr. Sims, to come down and speak with me. In April I received an offer to start in June. I now had to decide whether I wanted to travel the world or the State of Alabama.

Bitter or Better; it is your choice

I chose Alabama Power and I know God planned this path for me. I found out years later that Cullen had talked to everyone involved in the hiring process. He also had put in a strong endorsement of my family and background. Of course, when I tried to thank him, he just shrugged and said he had not done anything special.

I started with Alabama Power as a Junior Accountant in Tuscaloosa in June 1985. I progressed through various positions in the company while moving to Jasper and Demopolis. In 1998 I came full circle and returned to Tuscaloosa as the Business Office Manager. The next step would be Division Manager and then who knew what would happen.

I worked for and with some of the best people in the world during my career. Ms. Wade gave me my first supervisor position in Jasper and Mr. Maise gave me my first Manger position in Demopolis. Both people taught me so much about dealing with people and seeing the whole picture. My supervisor for 13 of my 20 years though was Mr. Bazemore. His influence is hard to measure. He made me keep the small things from becoming big. He was hard on me, but I knew he was preparing me to take his place one day.

I had achieved my dream. I was the boss. However, because of watching my dad and mom I made the commitment that I would be a co-worker and not the Boss. I wanted people to want to achieve our goals by setting the example and not cracking the whip. In the Air Force I had seen too many miserable people doing a job they did not like.

However, in June 2004 something was not right with my health. I had a severe catch in my neck that was so bad I constantly twitched to release the tension. At my uncle L.C. funeral, a cousin even asked me what was wrong. I had a ruptured disc repaired in 1996 so I just thought I had another pinched nerve. Then the fatigue started. I simply told myself this was because I was in my 40's and had been doing too much work around the property.

Then the night sweats started. Night sweats so bad that my sheets were soaked when I woke in the morning. I would wash the sheets every morning while I showered and dressed for work. As time moved into September all the symptoms merged, but I was already in trouble.

Just before the symptoms started, I had begun dating. We were moving along in our relationship, and I felt happy again. I broke the rule of not making major decision when in a health crisis. We were married the week before my treatments started. There was not enough foundation to hold the marriage together when the storm hit.

<u>Bitter or Better; it is your choice</u>

Kickoff

Of all the things in the world that made me go to the doctor was a hurricane! With my position as Office Manager also came the duties of Storm Trouble logistics. When a major storm would hit the area, my duties were to ensure lodging for out-of-town crews, arranging meals for all the lineman working to restore power and to supply snacks for the employees to have in their trucks.

Hurricane Ivan made landfall on September 16, 2004, just west of Gulf Shores, Alabama as a Category 3 storm. As the storm turned Northeast after landfall it caused extensive damage and large power outages from the Southwestern and Central parts of Alabama. My good friend Danny Glover was the Division Power Delivery Manager at the time. When power was restored, he was told to prepare crews to go South to aid with restoration efforts.

Bitter or Better; it is your choice

He asked me to travel with him to handle the logistics for our workers.

When I look back on the week, I came to realize that of the 168 possible hours, I had rested for 20! My body was so exhausted that I could hardly function. When we arrived back in Tuscaloosa, I made an appointment with my doctor. From the end of September and first of October I had many doctor visits, MRI's, CT, blood work, X-rays, PET scans and anything else he could think of. However, I wasn't fully prepared for the phone call of October 13, 2004.

My cell phone rang about 6:00 PM. and I could see it was from the doctor office. I thought, "finally I will get some answers." When I answered it was my doctor and not a nurse. Then instead of addressing me as Mr. Hood, like he always had done, I heard him start with Steven. My brain at once sent an alarm. Then he said the words that would change my life forever. “Steven, all your tests have come back. I am 99% sure that you have cancer!” Wait, what, did he just say the C word?

He told me he was sorry to break to me like this but that I needed to see an Oncologist as soon as possible. I asked when that would be set up. Then the alarm really went off; he replied, “you have an appointment at 9:00 in the morning! I thanked him, hung up the phone and just sat there. Silence, just silence and the thought of what had just happened.

I had Lyme’s Disease while I was in Demopolis. I was umpiring a Little League game when all the sudden every joint in my body felt like they were exploding. I had to take Rocephin by IV for a month to clear that from my body. The symptoms I were having were similar but much worse. I knew I was sick, but Cancer was not what I was ready for.

Bitter or Better; it is your choice

At this point I should tell you that very few people knew I was sick and seeing a doctor. My supervisor knew, my secretary Tracy Kelley knew (and bless her heart she covered for my absences so well) and my brother and sister. That was all I had even told I was not feeling well.

On the morning of Thursday, October 14, I went to see Dr Stidham at DCH in Tuscaloosa. I liked him immediately because he got straight to the point. He sat down in a chair next to me and said Mr. Hood, you have cancer, and it is at Stage 4B. I asked, "where is that on the scale" and he replied…" that is the end of the scale!"

He put the scans of my body on the screen, and he told me all the bright spots I saw was cancer. What I looked at the monitor it reminded me of a Christmas tree, I had bright spots all over my torso. I quit counting at 13 spots on my liver. My brain at once brought up how bad it was to have liver cancer.

Bitter or Better; it is your choice

For the first time (of several) I thought that I could die from this. He recommended that we needed to do some biopsies ASAP, so we needed to start Monday. I told him I needed a week to prepare, tell everyone what was going on and to but my affairs in order. He said OKAY and recommended that I check into hospital on Monday, October 25.

I drove the 40 minutes to my house in the country and started calling people. I called my brother Ron, sister Sharon, my cousin/brothers that are close to me Jerry, Jason and Brian, my close friends Danny Cooper, Roger Hall and Barbara Beavers, my children Joshua and Heather; but I just couldn't call my parents yet.

I got on my 4-wheeler and rode to an open spot and just laid there looking up at the clouds. I audibly said, "OK God, what happens now". I will never forget what happened next, because it was the first time, I heard God speak to me. Yep, right here some of you are going, yeah right! It wasn't a spoken voice, but I heard it in my head as clear as day. I had asked, what now, not why me. Because in my mind I thought why not me. I was glad it was me instead of my family or friends. Then He asked a simple question, "Do you trust Me?" Of course, Of course I trust you Lord. Then He replied "I will Heal you, but it will not be immediate. This will be a journey and you must Stay with Me."

In that instance, the fear of death left me. I no longer would be controlled but that emotion because I knew God was carrying me. Trust me, as you will read these pages, I was not always a magnificent, perfect, or positive Warrior. My prayer to God was simple, let me be a worthy Vessel.

I now had to call my parents. For some reason my mom and dad each had a landline phone beside their chair. I guess they didn't want to get up to answer the phone. Dad answered and I simply said tell mom to pick up on her phone. Now realize, they did not know I was sick and had been going to the doctor. They tried to chit chat and talk but I had to cut them off. I blurted out, "I have cancer, and it is bad!"

The scream of my mother still echoes in my head, "OH NO STEVEN" and she started sobbing. My dad said, "No Son it can't be", and he started crying. Over the next hour I consoled and comforted. They cried and asked questions; and I heard myself saying that I would be alright. I was going to beat cancer and I would be healed.

The next day I went into office early to talk with my boss. I told him what was going on and watched the shock in his face. I recommended I just could not work and had to get things in order. I then told my co-managers Tammy and Edna. I then had to recommend that they not tell anyone. I sent a note to all my coworkers in Customer Service and said we would have a meeting Monday morning at 7:00. Then I went home and sat in my recliner and cried… for most of the day.

The weekend was a blur with my parents coming to visit, I called more friends and family and assured each one of them that I was going to fight. On Monday morning, I looked in the faces of my team and broke the news. I told them I have cancer and will be going into hospital for tests and biopsies. I told them I was going to fight and that I planned to return in a couple of months. There is a song I heard that has a lyric, *IF you want to hear God laugh, just tell Him your plans*! He had to have snickered as I talked. Because He had an entirely different plan for me.

The rest of the week was coordination of my duties to other people and mostly taking phone calls and having people come to my office. It made me realize how many people cared and each one said they would pray. I told each person to flood Heaven with this request, *Heal Steven Hood*. I did not want, Lord if it be Your will, Lord help Steven through this. NO, I wanted Heaven to hear my name so much that God would tire of hearing it.

Then the most uplifting and amazing thing started. I was placed on prayer lists of churches all over town, all over the state of Alabama, all over the United States and even overseas!!! Realize I did not say I was placed on the Baptist church prayer list! I was prayed for my Methodist, Church of Christ, Church of God, Southern Baptist, Free Will Baptist, Missionary Baptist, and all other Faith's. My dear friend Danny Cooper is Catholic. He started praying Hail Marys for me twice a day, and he still does to this day.

On Monday, October 25, I was admitted for a biopsy of my right lung and lymph nodes. I woke up with stitches in my right side and a drain tube. The next day Dr. Stidham came by and said the lab results were inconclusive. So, we scheduled a biopsy of the liver. They gave me choice of being sedated and I was like, no I want to watch. So, during the liver biopsy I watched the monitor as the eight-inch needle went into my body. Then when surgeon was over a cancer spot, he extended a little claw like device that took a snip. He repeated on several areas, and I was taken back to my room.

The next day those results showed Carcinoma but no clear type of cancer. However, further tests showed cancer cells in my lymph nodes, kidney's, spleen, and gall bladder. I was falling behind and had not even started yet. It is a very weird feeling to know you need chemo. It destroys the good cells and the bad; but I knew the bad ones were still growing while nothing was being done to attack them.

Bitter or Better; it is your choice

While in the hospital I started seeing and feeling the love. One night I looked around and there were eight people in my room. What uplifted me was the background I had with each. Several were from Demopolis where we worked with Youth in our church. Couple were co-workers from Alabama Power. Plus, my family were there. I believe God was showing me I had a support group waiting to help.

I will always respect what Dr. Stidham did next. He referred me to Bruno Cancer Center at St Vincent's Hospital in Birmingham. Instead of acting like he knew everything he told me that he had done all he could do. I needed to be seen by someone with more knowledge and better facilities. The hospital administrator is a friend and he told me later that all he could say was I was a very sick man. It would take me a while to realize what this meant.

It was a week before my appointment, so I just hung out at home, and recovered from the biopsies. The chest tube getting pulled is not a fun event. Mom, dad, and Sharon came to visit. I thought walking would help me get my strength back faster. Sharon made the first of what would be many insights that I would need. She asked if I was sure I should be walking, that I might need that energy. Man was she ever correct.

I walked into the Bruno Cancer Center and met some of the most remarkable people. I also received the first affirmation from God that He was guiding this journey, I do NOT believe in coincidence. The doctor walked in and introduced himself as Dr. James Cantrell. My childhood best friend that I hiked, road bikes, played ball, went swimming, spent so much time with; his name is James Cantrell. This was the first of many signs to come that was God's way of telling me, "I Got This."

<u>Bitter or Better; it is your choice</u>

Chemo

The downward spiral of chemotherapy began quick. The number assigned to cancer means is it present in several areas or confined. One means just in a single area, and the number progresses based on spread of disease. The letter assigned of A means slow and B meaning aggressive of the growth of disease. My number of 4B was the worst rating because it meant several areas were already affected and it was growing fast. Dr Cantrell recommended that we start chemotherapy quickly to try and slow down the cancer.

I must give a side story at this point. Growing up my other sister (as I called her) was my first cousin Teresa. She was 6 months younger than me. We did everything together and she was the person I told everything. We grew up and started families and then she was diagnosed with cancer. I watched my sister fight and suffered more than I thought possible. At the age of 31 this sweet, precious, loving

Christian woman died. She left behind two children ages 8 and 4. I was so bitter that I swore I would never take chemo and if I got cancer, I would just let it kill me.

When Dr Cantrell finished talking, I heard myself saying "OK, when do we get started?" With God telling me to stay with Him, I prepared for the battle ahead. It was not that I needed to get things right with God. I honestly believe that the Power inside of me was just not going to sit down and let this cancer beat me.

Again, this was due to experiences in my life. My grandfather Walter decided he was dying at the age of 69. He sat down in his recliner and told everyone he was dying. He was truly a prophet because sure enough, at the age of 81 he died. 12 years of life was wasted just waiting on death.

I was admitted to the hospital after the second round of chemotherapy. Things were going awful. I was admitted but there was not a chair for someone to spend the night. The nurse said she would page Johnny. If there was a roll out cot anywhere in hospital, then he would find it. Around midnight someone knocked on my door and in walked Johnny. He set up the bed, put the sheets on and made sure everything was okay.

As he walked back by, he stopped at the foot of my bed. He asked if he could pray for me. Absolutely pray because I need all the prayers I can get. This 5-foot 2-inch, 120-pound, Black man did not pray; he talked to God! This man who I had never met brought the Holy Spirit into my room. He asked specifically for protection for Satan's attacks and for my complete Healing!

Here is where I went against all warning of do not make major decisions when dealing with a major issue. I made three major missteps throughout my battle. 1) I got married, 2) rewrote my will, and 3) sold my property (thanks IRS). I will not slam anyone; I am just telling facts. I was cared for while I was sick. However, I alienated my children and I have worked hard to try to repair since.

I am not going to get all medical with the chemotherapy used. You name it, and I took it. I do not want to call the names because they are like curses. When I first walked into Bruno Cancer Center, I thought it was a cold place. The front desk and lab staff were robotic in their work.

Boy was I ever wrong! I came to realize that it was their way of protecting themselves, because to get close meant heartbreak. I also figured out they wanted to see who would fight and follow instructions. The cancer seemed to jump to a new area with every visit.

On one appointment I was in intense pain. Highly likely the worse I have ever experienced. With every heartbeat it felt as nails were being driven into every joint in my body. I was screaming so loud they moved me into a room. This is when I saw the care in the nurses. The nurse I thought was the most distant was holding my hand with tears in her eyes.

This is my first introduction to a Bone Marrow Biopsy. A corkscrew contraption is pushed through your muscle. There is NO sedative for bone pain. With every turn I screamed. I was now tightly holding onto the headboard. I was screaming" it's like someone pounding nails into me." I heard, "now you know what I did for you." I no longer was screaming from pain; I was sobbing from guilt. It became so bad I was given liquid morphine.

Dr. Cantrell referred me to Vanderbilt Hospital for them to try and figure out what type of cancer I had. The resident that saw me had a cross lapel pin in his smock! February 24 is my DO NOT QUIT day. I had a spinal tap performed to see if spinal fluid would help with diagnosis.

Bitter or Better; it is your choice

I was despondent with not being able to find what cancer I had. This mystery cancer was out of control like a wildfire.

Early that morning, I was moving down a dark corridor. I was not walking but I knew I was moving. I was aware of something around me. Suddenly, I heard the Voice again. "What are you doing?" I am tired of fighting; I just want to come Home. "It is not time; we will come get you when it is time!" Then I was back in hospital bed. I did not tell anyone about this incident for at least a year. The worst physical days were still ahead of me.

They told me I would be there three days because movement might cause a spinal headache. I will never know why (probably insurance) but the next day the doctor asked if I wanted to go home. Well, of course I had rather be at home that a hospital. This was a terrible decision on my part.

Bitter or Better; it is your choice

On the drive home my head began to hurt. I have had sinus headaches, flu headache and even a concussion headache. NOTHING even comes close to a Spinal headache. By moving and riding 3 hours home in a car, my spinal fluid had leaked. I was in such intense pain by the third day that even the slightest noise was like an explosion. If someone opened a soda can it seemed like a shotgun blast. I went to the E.R. and begged the doctor to do something.

He then told me that they could go in and seal the area that was leaking. However, there would be a strong possibility that it could paralyze me! I said no thank you, received a prescription for stronger pain pills and headed home. It would be *eight* months before the headache truly went away.

I had a port placed in my chest to inject the poison (that is the only word I can use for chemo) because my veins collapsed. The cancer spread to my spleen and then I went from bad to worse. I will never forget that I went for a treatment but was unable to receive because my blood count and platelets were too low. I laid down on the couch to take a nap, I woke up in ICU with my brother about 6 inches from my face. He declared; well, we have good news 'They found a brain".

Now when you read what my brother said you may think that was tacky or crude. It told me that he was on my side. He was going to treat me normal which is what I craved from everyone! I could read the eyes of everyone that visited me. I could see Pity and I could see if someone thought I was going to die. However, I could also see the ones with Hope, and they would stand beside me through the fight. It was during the early stages I realized I was in the Mission Field. If you met me, you would hear about Jesus!

Bitter or Better; it is your choice

God sent confirmation by two ways. Shirley came for a visit and told me she felt led to tell me to spend my time praying for people. The following Sunday during sermon, the pastor said never shortchange prayer. He said during an event in his life someone had told them they were not physically able to help but they would pray. He said prayer is stronger and more beneficial than any physical help. You open Heaven when you pray.

I continued the regimen of chemotherapy, and the deterioration began slowly at first. I was naive to say the least. I felt fine the day after treatment and thought this is going to be OK. Then the third day came. The third day can only be described as Hell on earth. Everything smells bad, the taste disappears from food and the nausea is beyond anything you can imagine. I had food poisoning when I was younger, I would take it 10 out of 10 days over this feeling. The real joy was that each third day would get worse.

Bitter or Better; it is your choice

Because the cancer had spread from systemic to neurological part of body the doctor said we had to bend protocol. The clinic checks red blood count, white blood count and platelets. They want numbers to get to certain levels before giving you another round of poison. We did not have that luxury. When my blood numbers got to a level where they did not think I would die; I received a treatment for the alternating area. To give you a perspective, my platelets got as low as 7 and red count to 8!

During the worse part of my physical battle, an amazing uplifting event was done for me. All my belongings were still in Tuscaloosa. About twenty-five friends met on a Saturday, loaded a 26-foot U-Haul, and moved everything to Birmingham. Then they unloaded everything. My only regret was I could not be there to thank them. The spinal headache was in full bloom during this.

Bitter or Better; it is your choice

An infusion room is recliners along the wall separated by partitions. One day a patient was extremely mean to a nurse. She came to me next, and I could tell she wanted to burst into tears. I said, “you want me to go handle him?” She broke out a smile and said, “you would too if I would let you!” Do not be mean, rude, disrespectful to the people taking care of you. It is NOT their fault you are battling health issues.

The little things frustrate you if not careful. I could hardly function and the person next to me drove to their appointment. Some had the same cancer and did not look like me! Then Mel straightened me out. Even if two people have the same cancer, chemo does not react the same.

Another thing is please do not say, “well you look good.” We have a mirror! I wanted to hear, Keep Fighting, I am Praying, you will beat this, or how are you really feeling? Be Positive!

Bitter or Better; it is your choice

I started praying with the nurses. Over the years of my health issues there has not been a single person that refused a prayer. I would tell them I pray for them anyway. Then one day Mel was hooking me up for treatment. She looked at me and said, "you are going to make it." I wondered why she would say that. Then she finished by saying, "your attitude it going to carry you. Too many people feel sorry for themselves, but you do not"

I was told NOT to shave. A paper cut could cause me to bleed to death because my body would not be able to coagulate. During one hospital was stay the first of many occurrences. The nurse practitioner started coming into my room before she left for the evening. We were talking and she said, "something is different in this room." She was visiting so she would be refreshed. I knew then that the Holy Spirit was at work.

Bitter or Better; it is your choice

The plan was made to drill out a place in my head and to take a biopsy of the cancer on my brain. Also, they would implant a port so that chemo could be given directly into the neurological area. This device will never be removed because of the danger. So, after brain surgery was completed, I started the alternating chemo treatments.

During this time, my spleen enlarged so bad it was believed it would have to be removed. Then the very next day I received a diagnosis of my cancer. I had T-cell rich, B-cell enlarged non-Hodgkin's lymphoma with systemic and neurological involvement. We now knew the enemy name.

I was reminded God is never late, He is always on HIS time. Daniel would have liked for Him to show up before the lion's den. Shadrach, Meshach, and Abednego would have liked Him to show up before the furnace. God would not have received any Glory by doing it their way.

Bitter or Better; it is your choice

The chemotherapy treatments nearly killed me. Some people have asked me how I made it. I tell them I did not do anything but jump on Jesus' back and let Him carry me. The treatments made all my hair fall out. I lost 60 pounds and all the color in my skin. I had mouth sores from the roof of my mouth to my stomach. My veins collapsed from the poison going in my body. I had never had such pain and torment in my life. There were periods of time I did not pray for sleep; I prayed just for a little rest. To be honest, I prayed that He would let me come Home.

The best way to describe is to ask if you have ever had the true flu. Not the I feel bad but still go shopping the next day flu. The flu where it hurts to move, where light feels like it burns a hole in your head, where sound feels like your head will explode… you get the picture. Well, to describe the effects of chemotherapy; multiply that misery times 1,000. Then you are close to the ballpark of how bad it is.

The weird thing about these treatments was I knew I had to have them. The cancer was not taking a break, and neither could I. It was not like I looked forward to them. Trust me I dreaded each one more than the prior one. One day I went for a treatment and my numbers were just too low to safely administer. So, I went home depressed that I could not receive. Yes, depressed that I did not get poison injected into my body!!! I was told to come back the next day and we would try again.

While tossing and turning that night I was spiritually attacked by satan and his demons. When I say attacked, I mean audibly and visually. I do not tell anyone of what I saw and heard because I will not give the enemy a platform. I went through Ephesians 6 and mentally placed the Armor of God upon me. By 4:00 AM. I had not slept or rested. I knew the chances of receiving treatment were slim. I was whispering, "Jesus" over and over because that is all I could get out.

Then God sent a clear message to me. Suddenly at the foot of my bed was Teresa and L.C. Now I know this was not them, but I Believe it was two Angels sent to comfort me. If I had looked upon their real appearance I would have been petrified. No words were said but they sat down at the corners of my bed. I instantly fell asleep. I woke at 5:00 AM refreshed as if I had slept for days. I walked into the clinic at 7:00 and my numbers were at a safe level to receive my treatment.

During February and March 2005, I spent 29 of the 31 days in the hospital. This is another time that I was more dead than alive. I knew things had changed because the doctors were not in a hurry. They stayed longer than normal. Dr. Cantrell would even sit down and might stay 30 minutes to an hour just explaining everything. The No Visitor Sign was placed on my door. The outlook was bleak, but I held to God's promise that He would Heal me.

During this time two things happened that still trigger flash backs. The break room was across the hall. One night someone popped popcorn and hit 30:00 instead of 3:00. Just imagine the odor. Then two night later the coffee pot, with a small amount of coffee, was left on the burner. To this day strong coffee smell makes me nauseous.

While I lay on my death bed, I talked with God. Approximately 3 AM every morning I was woke up to be given medicines and blood to be drawn. This is so when the doctor starts rounds, they will have all the information needed. I never could go back to sleep, so God and I just talked. Too many times prayer is a check list of what we want from God.

However, when you talk it is a conversation. You wait for a response. Trust me, God will respond if you listen. He will answer every prayer. We want a Yes, every time; when sometimes the answer is No or Wait.

I want to try and explain what chemotherapy did to me. Everyone sees the hair fall out (and it falls out everywhere!) and the pale skin. However, most people do not see everything. The constant strain on me emotionally. I would pour everything I had into a visit; and collapse later.

Chemo messed up my digestive system so bad. I would be severely constipated for days. Then suddenly my system switch and I would have diarrhea for days. I learned to carry an extra pair or underwear and clothing. At some point I just lost my dignity and realized it was just part of the show.

Bitter or Better; it is your choice

The steroids I took made me crave food 24/7. I would be eating a meal and be thinking about what I would eat next. I carried a snack bag with me everywhere I went.

My heightened sense of smell made things hard to explain. After one treatment I was craving fish. We went through the drive thru and I opened the box to dig in. The smell hit me, and I nearly threw up. We had to stop to throw everything away.

Do not give flowers or wear perfume or cologne around chemo patients. The smell can cause instant nauseate, and you stay that way for hours or days. One reason I started sitting up front at church is due to the combination of scents. Being in front of the aromas was better that sitting behind.

Bitter or Better; it is your choice

Foul Ball

The most amazing thing was happening around me while I was at my lowest. The love of my friends and family lifted me above anything I could have imagined. Roger would come by once a week with lunch. I did not eat much but his fellowship inspired me to fight. I always cherished our friendship but my love and respect for him reached new heights. He would call at the exact time I needed a pick me up. I know God was using him to help me.

I was given Bible verse cards when I was first diagnosed. One of the cards had 2 Corinthians 12: 9-10 *And he said onto me, My grace is sufficient for thee: for My strength is made perfect in weakness. Most gladly therefore will I glory in my infirmities, that the power of Christ may rest upon me. Therefore, I take pleasure in infirmities, in reproaches, in necessities, in persecutions, in distresses for Christ's sake: for when I am weak, then am I strong. (KJV).*

Bitter or Better; it is your choice
Paul wrote this when begging God to remove the 'affliction' from him. This is my verse. I ask you to find your verse.

Also, I was given a CD of Crabb Family greatest hits. I have sung Through the Fire on my way too many a doctor appointment or hospital stay. The entire song is powerful, but the chorus is incredibly strong: '*Just remember when you're standing in the valley of decision, and the advisory says give in, just hold on, the Lord will show up, and He will take you through the fire again?"*[1]

Bruce Hutchins, a man who had been through a bone marrow transplant, would come see me every couple of weeks. He always assured me that the light at end of the tunnel was NOT a train! His most profound statement to

---

[1] Crabb, Gera (Crabb, 1999)ld. (1999) Through the Fire. On Crabb Family Greatest Hits (CD)

me was this “always remember that Cancer does not have a prayer”.

My cousin Jerry would come on Saturday morning with Chick-fil-A. He had a very busy life, but he fit me in somehow. He is a high school football coach and while I was battling cancer, he and his wife were trying to adopt children. If I was in the hospital, he found a way to come by and visit. He is one of the wisest people I know. His guidance and opinion are one that I always lean on.

My Aunt Shirley would come visit and bring me some fried pies. She would stay with me if I needed assistance. Just her being around always helped. She had watched Teresa go through this, so I know it brought back sad memories.

Mom and dad would love on me and do anything they could. They would always want to take me to eat or ride around. I hardly wanted to get out of my recliner! It was hard to explain that all I needed was companionship. I always felt like they were preparing for the worst. I don't blame them because I cannot imagine seeing your child in the shape I was.

My cousin Brian worked in retail in the jewelry business. His schedule is always at a frantic pace. I was told to accept help and not steal someone's blessing. When you are down and need help; let people help! One day while in hospital he called before coming over and asked if I needed anything. On this day I was craving (loads of steroids in my body) a Big Mac. When he walked in, I noticed the smile more than the sandwich. He was ecstatic that he could fulfill a wish for me. He also makes a great peanut butter sandwich!

Barbara was also used by God to pick me up. I always seemed to get a card or a call at just the right time She has always been more like a sister than a friend. She had the perfect words to help me get out of my funk. She and her husband Mal would stop by just for a visit. I always felt better and encouraged. She also worked with my friends Becky and Julia to put a scrap book together of my time with Alabama Power. I cannot explain how this book helped me. Looking at smiles and remembering was great medicine.

Jason became my financial rock during all of this. He also was a confidant and encourager. As if all my issues were not enough, the IRS decided it was a perfect time to audit. I could barely think, much less prepare for an audit. They were nice enough to come to my house. I sat at the table, but Jason did all the talking. Just for your information, they do not care if you are facing death.

My friend John Marchant went from being a friend to a very good friend. We worked together but usually just chatted over minor things. He would call to check on me, but then would allow me to forget my health issues for 30 to 45 minutes. He would tell me about his vacation trip. He would tell me about deer hunting or fishing. He would describe in such detail that I felt like I was out there with him.

Cooper, we always just called each other by last name, would contact me at just the right time. After the nap on couch and wake in ICU episode, word spread quickly that I was dying, Cooper thought he had to be with family. He and Lewis drove to Birmingham.

He said they walked into the waiting area, no one was there. His heart sank and he cautiously asked a nurse for news about me. She said, "he is in doing good and in ICU, do you want to see him." They walk in and I am sitting up eating Jell-o. He still tells me he has never been happier to see someone in ICU.

Bitter or Better; it is your choice

The main thing I want to stress is too be normal. Do not walk on eggshells. If I wanted to talk about the disease, I would bring it up. Talk to me like you always have. One good friend told me; you look terrible! We both laughed, which is what I needed.

Then there was my brother Ron and sister Sharon. They became my support through the toughest time. Ron traveled with his job and was on the road a lot. Somehow his route would bring him by for a visit. He lived three hours away but would somehow end up at the hospital on his way home. He always said he was just taking a different route. He suggested I re-read the book of Job. I had avoided because of the multitude of issues he went through. There it was in Job 1:6 and again in Job 2:1 *There was a day when the sons of God came too present themselves before the Lord, and Satan came also among them.*

Bitter or Better; it is your choice

God is the one that asked, "Have you considered my servant, Job?" Before Satan could do anything, God had to give him permission. The only limit He set was that he could not kill Job, I hope you understand what I did that day. Once you accept Jesus, do you not also give Him your life? Let God get the Glory during the situation you find yourself. Someone needs to see that your Faith is strong in the valley, just as it is on the mountain top.

Realize that if you are a Christian, this is as close to Hell as you will get. Also, this is as close to Heaven as a non-Believer will get. Earth is not my home. All of us are just passing through.

How could I have read the Bible and missed this? I am not comparing myself to Job, but suddenly these verses spoke to me. I was not getting picked on or punished, God was Trusting me. I had asked to be His Vessel and He was using me. The Spirit inside me became bolder than ever. I quit walking through situations and starting walking in situations. I feel a responsibility to honor that Trust.

There were so many instances that the Holy Spirit would lead me to talk to a person. Time after time I was thanked for listening and praying with someone. To this day the inside joke between Ron and I is when he will ask me, "remind me, why are you still here?"

Sharon was the prophet throughout. In any situation she gave such deep Spiritual advise. She came every week on her off day from work. I know the trip was not easy, but I cannot express how she was used by God to help me. I respect her so much. The day would pass quickly and all we did was talk or sometimes just sit and be quiet.

Another thing I recommend is lose the negativity. I learned to let a caller leave a message. Then when I returned the call, I was in control of ending the call. Also, you do not have to call everyone. This is a time to get selfish and think of yourself. A big motivation for me was the Jim Valvano 'Never Give Up' speech and Dr S.M. Lockridge sermon 'That's My King'. I cannot count the number of times I watched each. Also, listen to uplifting and inspirational music.

Then in May of 2005, I was able to attend my son's high school graduation, I doubted if I would be alive, much less able to walk into the auditorium. I had achieved another goal I had set. However, the biggest news was the doctors declared me cancer free in June 2005. Unfortunately, this is when my marriage began showing problems. As my health improved, my marriage got worse.

Becky and others planned for me to attend an afterhours company function. Getting to see so many friends helped me so much. I realized it helped them too. There were drawings for door prizes. First Billy and then

Rex brought me their prizes. All I could do was cry. To be so humbled by their words and actions still affect me.

Jim Key was another vital person on my team. He had battled cancer and was in remission. He came by once a week with lunch. He answered all my questions, and I had a lot of them. Most of the time we just talked. He hid from me that he had begun feeling bad. I think to protect my outlook. Then one day I discovered he was in the hospital. A week later he entered Heaven. At his funeral I told his widow that I would fight for both of us. I still am to this day.

I was able to slowly get out of the house/ I celebrated my 45th birthday with family and friends. I was slowly gaining strength and stamina back. Then one day I fell while leaning over to put something in the dishwasher. I thought, no big deal, I am just clumsy.

Bitter or Better; it is your choice

Then a few days later, I fell again. I called Dr. Cantrell office and of course was told to come in immediately. I was admitted and the MRI revealed that cancer had returned in three areas on my spine.

I wanted to scream. I wanted to be mad. I wanted to know why? So, I did ask God why. Do not ever ask God why if you are not ready for the response. Read Job 38 if you need a refresher." I did not declare the journey over, just stay with Me!"

We were having a Hood cousin reunion just two days later, so I had to break the news. I remember telling them I did not know if I had the fight in me to go through chemo again. By Monday I had gotten over my pity party and knew I was ready.

That is another rule that my team knew about me. When I had a setback or bad news, I had a one-day wallow rule. I might whine and be down on things. However, it could only last 24 hours. Then the next day it was back to the fight.

It is funny how two people can say different things but motivate you the same. Jerry told me it was like baseball. “You hit one deep and thought it was a home run, but it curved at the last minute for a Foul Ball.” Jason put it blunter, “good because I was going to kick your ass if you tried to quit.”

Dr. Cantrell did something that I will respect him for as long as I live. He honestly said he had done all he could. He made an appointment with Kirklin Clinic of UAB for me. He said they were better equipped to figure out what was going on in my body.

Bitter or Better; it is your choice

UAB

With my first appointment I met Dr Peter Emmanuel and Dr. Forero who would be my Oncologists. I had also been given an appointment with Dr. Burt Nabors who would be my Neuro Oncologist. I felt comfortable with them immediately. This is especially important for any patient. There are many great doctors and hospitals. Find the one that you feel at ease with. I have been with UAB for all my care since October 2005 and have no regrets.

Dr. Nabors would take the lead since it was my neurological system under attack. The cancer had exploded with tumors on my upper, middle, and lower spine. This is where the High Dose Methotrexate comes in. This is by far one of the nastiest things I had put in my body.

Before the regimen began, there was a trip to Las Vegas. I was just site seeing and preparing for chemo. Around 4 AM the phone rang in my room. It was Heather telling me Joshua had been in a serious accident. He had been found lying in the road by two men on their way to work. No one knew how long ago the wreck happened.

We decide we must get back to Alabama, and we had 90 minutes to get packed and reach the airport. When we get out of the cab the bellhop checked our bags and notified my Gate. Someone was waiting with a wheelchair to get me to the terminal. They told my spouse to take carry on and go on the departure gate.

This young man took me through screening, back corridors and other shortcuts. At one checkpoint a passenger started complaining about me cutting the line. He kept mouthing off, so I slowly stood up. I was a foot or taller. I looked down at him and simply said, “I pray Stage 4 cancer never ravages your body, and then you find out your son has an auto accident.” The look on his face was priceless.

Bitter or Better; it is your choice

We practically are running now as we reach the correct Terminal. Of course, my gate is at the far end. He is yelling for people to move and not slowing down. As I approach the Gate, the airplane has been held ten minutes and I must hurry. (I find out later the pilot had been pushed back but retuned because of my emergency.) I am rolled all the way to the door of aircraft. I stand up and turn to thank the young man. I look at his name tag. His name is Angel.

We finally arrive in Birmingham and drive to the hospital. Thank God my son is not seriously injured. I decide to stay overnight just to make sure he is ok. God had someone waiting on me in waiting room.

My friend and is sitting there with her two sisters and her mother. Her dad is in serious condition, and they are of course upset. One of her sisters made a statement that allowed me to Witness. She said that they did not believe her dad even knew they were there.

Bitter or Better; it is your choice

I am going to tell you what I shared with her. We know you are there. We may not communicate but we hear everything. It may be more that I sensed someone. Talk to your loved one laying there in the bed. There were times that I could not talk, due to either pain medicine or the pain itself; but I could tell them later who had been in my room. I went to the wake a week or two later. All the family thanked me for the advice. They had talked and laughed at old adventures. They had been able to say their goodbyes and felt as if he knew how much he was loved.

The plan was for to be admitted on Monday, October 5. An IV with fluids would be started and the then the chemo started. When the chemo finished, IVs were continued until my toxicity was below a certain level. This stuff so nasty. I had to be weighed and the dose calculated on each treatment. I would not be discharged until that level was met. I would then have a week off and we would repeat.

I received 20 (yes TWENTY) IV bags before I was discharged. I returned on October 19 to repeat the process. Let me tell you what 20 bags of fluid does to you. You urinate, a LOT. I placed a urinal next to my bed and recliner and one in the car. There was no urge or warning. The countdown started at three and you better be ready.

This treatment is very dangerous for your kidneys, hence all the fluids. All my urination shredded the inside of my bladder. I looked at the scan and it looked like someone had taken a knife and carved it up. While I was in hospital, we worked out a system to have three urinals by my bed. I could barely move to get on my side. I would have two filled between the time I pressed the call light, and the nurse would come in.

Bitter or Better; it is your choice

Every two weeks it was the same drill. I honestly did not sleep during this entire time. Let that soak in, for three months I was sleep deprived. I dosed or napped fifteen minutes at the most. Now this really took a toll on my body. I was Mentally, Emotionally and Physically exhausted. During this time, I was also evaluated and placed on the Bone Marrow Transplant List. Just a side note; I found out that the spinal fluid drawn back in February 2004 that gave me an eight-month spinal headache - it was never even evaluated!!!!

I want to point out that I had been placed under the care of each department Head. I laughed and told them that I wanted a percentage of any royalties they made by telling my story. Dr. Emanuel was the only one that wanted to slow down. He saw something in my numbers that showed my body was Healing. What they all did not know was that I was through.

Bitter or Better; it is your choice

When discharging me on December 16, 2005, I told them there would be no future treatments. I had twenty-two chemo treatments within 13 months and my body and mind was finished. I told them all that I had the Great Physician on my case. He would make decision if cancer would kill me or not. When I left the hospital, I was a very sick man. It would take the doctors months to realize what I already knew – I was Healed!

The strange thing about knowing you are Healed is that everyone else does not accept it. Most but not all people that is. Roger, Barbara, Becky, Jason, Jerry, Brian, Ron, Danny, John and Sharon did. There were others, but these people were my team. I had a family friend ask my mom did she think I had really had cancer! The process of recovery still takes a long time. My body was a wreck and still is. The thing about chemo is the only way to flush it out is to urinate it out. The problem is you cannot urinate that much.

I began physical therapy to try and regain stamina and balance. The son of my co-worker Valerie, gave me a small cross to carry in my pocket. I always had it in my pocket when walking into therapy. One day I came out and it was gone. I went back and searched the rooms I was it. I checked my truck and to my dismay it was gone. Several weeks later I got in my truck to go to therapy, the cross was on my console. I asked and no one had put it there. It was just another sign.

During recovery I started having prostate issues. In April 2007 I was referred to Urologist a TURP and TUNA were done to take a biopsy. Take my word, neither are very pleasant. Out of 13 samples taken there were two that came back positive. So, know I have prostate cancer and we go over all the treatment options. I told the doctors we would do nothing. Of course, that was met with not much enthusiasm. However, I knew that it was just another Spiritual attack. I never had a treatment and the PSA levels have always been in normal range.

I want to point out something to anyone that may be going through a crisis. Life is busy so do not let the lack of attention bother you. When you are near death, everyone pauses and works you into their schedule. Just to be honest, after a year the expectation is you are back in the game of life, or you are dead. As Cooper put it best," Hell Hood, a lot of people that saw you just Thanked God it wasn't them".

Another major issue I started to notice was that most people cannot truly understand the pain you go through. Then I realized the worst level of pain that anyone can understand, is the worse pain they have ever had. Telling someone just how bad it hurts to simply move cannot be explained to someone who has only dealt with a toothache. Do not take it personal, just love on them and do not let it bother you. If level four is as bad as they have ever had then you cannot explain a level 84.

Please do not ever tell someone, "I know how you feel" You do not! The same issue or crisis may arise, but it is different for every person. I tell people I am here to listen, if you ever need to talk.

Also, being the center of attention is intoxicating. I guess I understand why some athletes have a tough time going into normal activities. When I have been sick, everyone has been there. It was up to me to adjust back to a day-to-day routine. The cards do not come as often, the call and text messages slack off. This isn't a sign you have been forgotten; it just means you are back into the flow of life.

The doctors did not take my word for it, so I kept having appointments. MRI's, CT's, PET scans, x-rays,

Bitter or Better; it is your choice

DEXA scans and if you can name it, I have had it. Every scan kept coming back with scar tissue or shrinkage of area. I just smiled and worked the Mission field. Dr. Emanuel left and Dr Forero became my primary Oncologist. This man became more than a doctor, he became my friend. I worked hard throughout 2006 and 2007 to get back in some sort of shape to return to work.

Next Chapter

I kept myself busy. I did PT, I walked, I volunteered at church, and I visited friends and family. I remember one of the first outdoor events I attended was a youth baseball game for Alex, Roger's son. It felt so good to be outdoors. The next event was a soccer game for Roger's daughter, Rachel. I leaned on Roger even more and our bond became even closer. We have been friends thirty years and have never had a cross word. We hold each other accountable and that is something we both cherish.

I went to see my parents as much as I could. Now when they came, we went out to eat. Sharon would come for a visit and Ron still managed to have his route home include a stop to see me.

I would drop in and visit Barbara. She always lifted me up. Her outlook inspired me to keep working and keep moving. Occasionally I would go by the office to see friends. However, it was simply different. Personnel had changed and I was now the "who is that guy" hanging around the office.

Charles had not filled my position in the months I had been fighting. I take that as a huge compliment because he knew I needed a goal to reach. The highest compliment he had was when he told me, "You don't know what you had, until it is gone." I called and told him that it was time that the office moved forward. I asked Tracy and Barbara to box up all my personal stuff. Mike Porter drove me over for me to gather the boxes.

Mom's little saying echoed in my ears as everyone had to come give me a hug, a handshake or to say hello. One of the highest honors I have ever received once given to me by Mike Ford. Mike worked outside collecting and was under union classification. He asked to be able to come load my boxes in the car. He shook my hand and said,

Bitter or Better; it is your choice

"Steven, when you got here you told us that your priority was Faith, Family and then work. You showed that every day." I could not help but cry and thank God, He had been using me all along." There was a note over the light switch to not turn off the lights. They had left the light on the entire time I was gone. I turned it off as I walked out.

At doctor appointments there always seemed to be someone to talk to. I could feel the Holy Spirit nudge me. I would simply introduce myself, sit down and ask if everything was okay. I would listen and then tell them a brief history. On more than one occasion I had them go get their family member and proclaim, "he is cancer free; you have to fight because you can beat it too."

I finally got a meeting with an executive with Alabama Power. I was able to convince that I was ready to return. In my feeble mind I still thought this was my goal in life. After this I was scheduled to meet with Alabama

Bitter or Better; it is your choice

Power nurse and H.R. I knew these people, so we were having a relaxed meeting. The turning point still burns in my head. They were taking notes and I was asked what medications I was taking. As I was talking the nurse put down her pen and then asked me, “did you drive yourself today?”

The entire meeting turned 180 degrees at that point. We kept talking but they were no longer taking notes and seemed ready to wrap it up. I got home and called the nurse and asked, “the company does not want me back does it?” She started the company line and exposure and I just stopped her. “Yes, she said, it would be too great of a liability since you work with customers.” I heard the door shut, locks closed, and key thrown away. My career was officially over.

It took me years to realize that I went into deep depression that day. Of course, I told very few people. That is what depression does. It makes you think people will look at you differently. I finally told Cooper one day how worthless I felt. His words stay with me, “Hood, you are alive, that is a gift! The Lord wants you to do something else.”

The marriage ended really when I was placed on permanent disability from Alabama Power. It was completed in early 2007. There is nothing bad to say. There was just separation during the time it looked like I was going to die.

I moved to Tuscaloosa to be around my children I had a short-term lease on an apartment and thought this would help me gather my thoughts. What it did was make me more withdrawn and depressed. My children were adults and had lives of their own. I love my children, but something changed during all this time. I would find out what had caused it.

Bitter or Better; it is your choice

I had been isolated. Years later I found out my children, friends and others would call to check on me. I was never given the message from certain people. I thought I was abandoned, they thought I did not need them.

I was then placed on Leave of Absence – Permanent Disability by Alabama Power. Since April 2005 I had been drawing Social Security and from private disability policies. Another example for God taking care of me had happened years before and I had forgot. Roger had asked if I had bought Supplemental disability since I was considered highly compensated. When I had moved to Tuscaloosa in 1998, I did indeed check the box. I had been paying a small premium that would now make a huge difference in my life.

Depression is a lie from Hell. It leads you to focus on what you lost instead of what you have gained. I was closer to God than ever in my life. I had so much to be

Thankful for. Instead, the demons whispered in my ear and started to sway. Before this I had never understood why Elijah ran; after God had just destroyed the followers of Baal at Mt Carmel (1 Kings 18:20- 1 Kings 19-3)

Satan is a liar, deceiver and works to cause disharmony in God's plan. That is what he and his demons do all the time. They are not this cartoon depiction of horns and a spiked tail. Satan was the music director in Heaven. He was beautifully adored before God cast him out. Satan is that car you must have, that career that becomes so important or just about anything can be done to separate you from God. My co-worker, Audrey Vaughn, told me once; "Jesus had to tell him to leave three times, why do you expect him to listen to you the first time."

I then started to put out a verbal fleece as Gideon had with an actual fleece. (Judges 6:37-40) I needed a location because I was going to copy Elijah and run. I did not want to be around anything that reminded me of job I lost, land I had to sell (the IRS did not go easy on me), or my failed relationships. Location after location just did not work out.

I went to see a friend who had started a new church. The fleece was if he was there, I was to stay in Tuscaloosa. He was not there. My message to call me was never returned.

Ron and family lived in Batesville Mississippi. I went for a visit and asked my sister-in-law to just drive me around town. I put a fleece to God, if there is a house for sale on Church Street, then I know you want me to move here. She had lived in Batesville 25 years and did not even think there was a Church Street. We did not drive two blocks and guess what street we intersected with? There in plain view was a For Sale sign in the yard! I knew a total of three people, but I moved in 2007. You want to know the best part; God was there waiting.

Renewal

I had the moving company deliver my belongings to Watt Street. I had gone to my cave, farther in the desert. I even had the absolute nerve to tell God I was going to find a church but was not going to become involved. In His absolute Glory I wonder if He thought, oh yeah, watch this.

During the next couple of years my great nephew, Deandre 'Dre' LeRon Taylor became vital to me. I love this young man. He has the kindest spirit and becomes my best buddy. When Sharon had a day off, they would come to Hackleburg. I would drive over and spend the day.

Dre and I would build stuff in the shop. We caught a snake that was under my parents' house. We watered flowers and did basically whatever he wanted. The most important thing Dre did was give me a sense of purpose.

I found a church or more like it found me. It was and still is led by Dr. Paul Middleton. He was used to restore my outlook, for the chains of my past to be broken and to be ready to be used by God, more than anyone along this journey. It was now 2007 and I had to get moving again.

Ron told me that a friend of his had suffered a massive heart attack. I went to the hospital to visit and sort of joined the family. I know that God wanted me there to encourage Doug Wiggs to fight. He and his dad were farmers and in the waiting room they were talking about Doug would not be able to drive. I became the driver for Mr. Doug. More than being a driver I found a dear and special friend.

Bitter or Better; it is your choice

One Sunday morning I decided to visit a church near my house. The moment I walked into the doors of Calvary Baptist Church, I heard "this is where I want you." I moved my letter on the third service I attended. The people were marvelous, but I truly felt Jesus throughout everything that was done. I got to know several people and settled in nicely to attending church and going home.

Then one Sunday, this knucklehead teenager (I love you Steve'O) walked up to me and asked if I would want to be their Sunday school teacher. I told him I was flattered but there was already a teacher, and it would have to be approved by the pastor and others. Steve matter of fact said, "oh the teacher had rather be assistant instead of lead and I already talked to Brother Paul" I thought to myself, so much for not getting involved.

I became a youth Sunday school teacher, was active in Men's Brotherhood, part of the Prayer team and helped set up a Counseling program for new Believers. I loved every moment, but I loved more being mentored by my pastor, Paul Middleton. I started online classes through Liberty University to pursue my Master's in Pastoral Counseling. Brother Paul had his Master's in Counseling and was pursuing his Doctorate. God had it all worked out.

Paul helped me forgive myself. I was the one still clinging to things that satan could use against me. He taught me how to listen to people and focus on what they needed. It wasn't about me or my experiences. I could relay what God had done for me in certain situations if needed. By doing this I once again had a purpose. I felt like the dirt of guilt and regrets were washed away.

The only fault my pastor had was he is an LSU fan. I must admit I enjoyed wearing my Alabama shirt on certain Sunday's.

Bitter or Better; it is your choice

Meanwhile I drove Doug everywhere he needed to go. Three days a week we went too Oxford for Physical Therapy. I learned roads and shortcuts all over the Delta of Mississippi. We went for tractor parts from Arkansas to Memphis to Central Mississippi. With all that riding a brotherhood was formed. We had a lot in common with our personal lives but so much more with our believes and life situations. Between my cancer and his heart trouble there was a lot to talk about.

Most of the time we talked about our Faith. We would talk about scripture or a Sunday school lesson. Doug has this way of just cutting through the garbage and getting to the point. I remember one day he reminded me that God had forgotten about things and why did I keep holding on to them. That helped me realize to just leave it alone once God had forgiven me.

Bitter or Better; it is your choice

When we were discussing something and needed clarification, we would call Brother Larry. He was pastor at Doug church but was a dear friend. Brother Larry had a deep insight into the Bible and was an outstanding man. Cancer has since claimed Brother Larry body, but he was freed into his Heavenly body.

After I was Healed, I tried to reduce the alimony payments from my first marriage. I did not do this to be spiteful, but my financial condition had dramatically changed. Even though I was at 50% income from time of decree, the judge only slightly reduced the monthly payment.

If not for Ron and Doug, I would have gone hungry. On Sunday afternoon I would eat with Ron and family. leftovers would go home with me for supper. Wednesday night after church would be Sonic. During the week, Doug paid for most meals as we traveled around. Supper on many occasions would be limited.

I was still going to Birmingham for checkups with my doctors. One day Dr Forero walked in and said, “what are we going to do about these hips.” Now he was my Oncologist, but he was looking out for my total well-being. He then informed me that the chemo in my body was causing deterioration of both hips. I was referred to a surgeon and was told that both hips needed work.

Instead of going straight for surgery, I decided to see a doctor about cortisone shots. This is the only doctor that failed me. I was in room waiting on a shot. The nurse came in and prepared the shot and then set it down on the table. When quack came in, I ask him about it being uncovered. He just shrugged it off. Like an idiot, I let him insert in needle in me. I was diagnosed with MRSA staph infection a week later.

Bitter or Better; it is your choice

When I had first moved to Watt Street, the neighbor little boy came over to visit. That led me to his mom. We talked one day about her relationship with God. She used to go to church but had just drifted away. I went to the local Christian bookstore and bought her a Bible. I would make sure she was reading every time I saw her.

With MRSA I was confined to the house. However, I had a church, friends, brother, and neighbor to help me. I have a flesh scar on both hips from the procedures. I filed a complaint with Alabama Board of Medical Examiners. My response said no neglect was found but they would keep on file.

After the MRSA cleared, I made one of the bone head, dumbest, idiotic decisions I have ever made. I decided to have both done at the same time. I was hurting so bad that I thought suffer all at once and get it done. I had bilateral hip resurfacing in September 2008. Hip resurfacing is where the socket part of hip is replaced but the femur bone is not. I had immobilized myself.

Because I lived alone, I had to stay in rehab center for several weeks. Once again, I was placed in situations to talk to patients and staff about Jesus. There were Aides who had immigrated from India. I spoke about being Healed by Jesus and my personal relationship. They listened so I sowed seeds.

One day a nurse came in and I could tell something was wrong. She said was just having issues with teenage son. I asked if I could pray with her. When we finished praying, she had tears in her eyes. She thanked me for taking the time to pray. I realized that I was being placed among people that mind never attend church or might not hear the great news of Jesus. It was just reaffirmation this was my Mission Field. God was using me to reach people. It was not about my health.

Bitter or Better; it is your choice

Unfortunately, I cannot say I was the perfect patient. A lot of issues boiled over and I wanted to go home. I send a group text for someone to get me. It was a three-hour trip, but I did not care. Jason came to calm me down. He talked to the nurse and then laid out the facts of me leaving. When he finished, he told me "You do not want to do that." It was not a suggestion. He was telling me I was not going anywhere.

I just needed someone to take charge for me because I had lost all control. Roger came shortly afterwards. We had a frank discussion about what was really bothering me. He of course helped me see the big picture. I had to take care and get healthy. That was my only priority!

In therapy room one morning, God sent another person in my path. It isn't hard to see the outward signs of chemo, but I pick up on little things that tell me how a person feels. There was this young woman wearing a head scarf and she spent most of therapy time as far away from group as possible. She scanned the room more than focusing on her exercise. If you made eye contact, she would quickly look away.

I made a point of rolling over in wheelchair and I think I complimented how pretty her scarf was. Then I asked, "how many treatments did you have?" Before she could say anything, I told her my hair had fallen out twice over my 22 treatments. Then I just listened as she told me her story. She thanked me for our talk. I know she felt better because someone that related had taken the time.

When I was discharged, Doug was now the driver. I ended up staying in his spare bedroom while I recovered. I especially grew close to his son Kyle. He has a Spirit about him that is wonderful to see. Doug's parents lived next door and they just adopted me into the family.

Bitter or Better; it is your choice

Later, Doug suffered a setback during a procedure to clean out a stint. We waited all day for the doctor to come by and give us results. About 6 PM the doctor walked through the door and declared, “I was unable to repair the stint, your heart is in bad shape, and we are sending you to Memphis!”

The room went completely silent, and the doctor turned to just walk out. I guess because I had been in hospital so much I just spoke up. “When is he going?” “What do you mean is heart was too bad?” What is Memphis going to do that you can’t?”

That gave time for the shock to where off and then Doug and family started asking questions. We kept an uncomfortable doctor for 10 minutes making him answer questions. Then I saw one of the most sincere, heartfelt prayers I have ever heard. We held hand around Doug and

Alabama Power

Roger M. Hall
General Shops Manager
Power Delivery

744 Highway 87
Calera, Alabama 35040
205 664 6059 tel
205 541 8575 cell
rmhall@southernco.com

er or Better; it is your choice

e begged Jesus to not take his dad, that he needed him!

vas 8 at the time, he is now 21 and in college!

Ron is good friends with the Director of non-profit h supports a school in Honduras. I was able to go on a on Trip with a team in early 2009. When we landed in San Pedro Sula, you notice the difference right away. There are soldiers with their machine guns patrolling. I was prepared to have all my documents ready and understood not to mess around in any way. The 8-hour van ride is a wakeup call at the absolute poverty.

New Vision runs a ministry for children high in the mountain region. The facilities are enclosed with razor wire topped fence with one gate. At night outside security is stationed. Dr. Garrot is a dentist so free dental care is provided. Medicines and clothing had been shipped ahead and the pharmacist on Team dispersed those. Donated clothing had also been shipped. We spent the first night sorting them to disperse. Word had spread that we were coming.

The gates will open at 8 AM. At 6:30 there are close to a hundred in line. Group presentation of the Gospel is the first thing each person attends. Others and I are filling one pound bags with rice and beans. The real prize for each person is their own Bible.

I have 5 Bibles with various translations. These people have walked miles to receive one! There are Spanish speaking pastors with us. I do not understand what is being said, but the Joy of accepting Jesus does not need an interpreter.

Later as I give out a bag of rice and bag of beans, I start to give to a woman. She stops me to let me know she is with the person I just gave some to. I tell her “For you”, she starts to cry and thanking me. I still cherish the hug.

Bitter or Better; it is your choice
There are people everywhere with tears in their eyes and holding the Word of God!

We were so far up the mountain that we were above the clouds. I have never seen so many stars. There is no artificial light to block to compete, so it is the most breathtaking site. The team has a Bible class and prayer every night. We only stay four days, but I came down that mountain a different man that the one that went up.

By the Winter of 2009, I felt like I was going to move back home. I had received my Masters in Pastoral Counseling from Liberty University and had a different mindset. My parents were both getting in poor health. With Ron and Sharon, both working it just made sense to move back home. Yet another God thing because I had told Teresa when we were in high school. *I am moving away from here and never coming back*. Then God sent Sharon

Kay aka Sherry into my life. I didn't plan on remarrying, but God knew I needed a partner.

I hated to leave my brother behind because we had gotten closer. I hated to leave Doug because he had become my brother. I had become close to his mom and dad but especially to Kyle. I am forever grateful for my time in Mississippi. I thought I was running but God was preparing me.

Bitter or Better; it is your choice

Home and Starting Over

I have known Sherry since elementary school. My parents and hers were friends. I never dated her in high school but now God had placed her into my life. We first dated just before my Honduras trip. We were married in July 2010, I started volunteering with the high school baseball and football program as Statistician, and reconnected with friend and now brother-in-law, Rob Randolph.

I have known the coach my entire life. Coach Hudson will never know how much it helped me being around the athletes. It helped keep me active. I had something to do. I felt like I had a purpose. I started getting their stats in the area newspaper. That is something I would have liked when I was in school. Everyone likes a little attention!

It also allowed me to be someone who would listen. Coaches must be demanding because their job is to win games. I was able to listen to their problems, their troubles and sometimes to encourage. I always told them that when a coach quits yelling at you is when you worry. That means they have given up on you. I told each athlete, "I will not divulge anything you tell me, unless it might cause harm to you or someone else.

Rob and I piddled a couple of days a week. He had made poor decisions in his life and was looked down on by the residents of Hackleburg. I know this firsthand. When we pulled up to local convenience store there were a group of men inside drinking coffee. The store fell quiet as we opened the door and stayed that way. When we got back in truck you could see the talking start up. I wanted to go tell them off, but Rob said no just ignore them. I waved as we left.

Rob was hungry to learn the Bible. Every time we were together, he had question after question about meaning of certain scripture. He made me stronger because I had to be prepared. I realized so many people did not want to forgive Rob, but it was not up to them.

Rob lived with guilt of not being there for his family. One day he explained just how the devil worked against him. When he went to bed he would cry and swear he was through and would never do again. He said no matter what time he woke up, his brain made him crave and go right back in the filth.

As he lay on his prison bunk one night he cried to God, "Lord please forgive me and take this away." Instantly he had a feeling go through his entire body. He told me, "Right then I knew I was forgiven, and the craving was gone." I remember telling him that satan hated me, but he despised him.

A local pastor was pressuring him to come forward during a service so he could make public. Rob said he just felt like he wanted a show. Rob had accepted Christ as a teenager and was baptized. He had just led satan pull him down the wrong path.

One day I just blurted out, "Rob, if you died right now would you be in Heaven or Hell. Without hesitation, he answered "Heaven." I stated that the matter seemed settled to me. If someone hesitated when answering I reacted differently. From that day he had a Peace. Rob died of massive heart attack on April 10, 2011. I was honored to speak at his funeral.

April 27, 2011 is the deadliest tornado outbreak in the State of Alabama. TV meteorologists for days warned us to take this seriously and be prepared. Sherry and I went to the storm shelter at three times by 12:30 that afternoon. Sheets of hail had fallen each time like a trial run. When we got home about 1 PM, Sherry had made the remark that she would just stay home if another warning was issued.

Bitter or Better; it is your choice

About 3:15 the meteorologist on TV was showing a tornado hit Cullman. You could hear someone off screen say there is a tornado warning in Marion County. That was our county! Then the weather alarm on iPhone went off. On TV the report was a tornado in the Hamilton area. I yelled to Sherry to get in the car and call our daughter Erin to meet us at storm shelter.

I was thirteen when an F4 tornado hit the town of Guin in the southern part of Marion County. I have been weather interested ever since then. I knew tornados follow a SW to NE directional path. Hamilton is SW of Hackleburg, so I knew it was headed toward us. We ran outside to jump in the car, and I glanced South. What I saw can only be described as pure evil.

The tree line blocked the bottom of the storm. It seemed as if the entire sky was moving. I could see objects, so it was probably within 1-2 miles of where I stood. There was the deep greenish hue which meant debris. There was also an ugly yellowish tint. Orange and reddish streaks mixed in as well.

I jumped in car and drove ahead of it for the three miles to Sherry's parents' house. Their neighbor has a storm shelter and as we jumped out about 15 people were just standing looking toward where we had come from. I told everyone to listen, there was no sound of a cat, dog, frog, cricket, or bird. There was just dead silence and a heaviness in the air.

I told everyone to get in the shelter. All of us crammed into the storm house. I still remember the latch being closed and two men holding it down to stay in place. The pressure placed on your eardrums is enormous. It is worse than taking off or landing in a jet airliner. It was even difficult to move your jaw to make your ears pop.

Bitter or Better; it is your choice

Then the sound. That terrible sound! Some people relate it to a train. I relate it more to group of angry hornets, multiplied several hundred times. Yes, I have had to jump into a creek to avoid an angry bunch off hornets. It is not a good sound. It seemed like it lasted minutes, but really was over in seconds.

I remember looking at Sherry and telling her we would not have a home when we got out of the shelter. She did not want me to think so negatively. I knew it was not a thought. When we left the shelter, I strangely noticed how fresh the air seemed. I looked toward the Northeast and knew Phil Campbell was about to get hit. The neighborhood had slight damage and I could see some tree damage. We hadn't driven a quarter mile and the destruction was obvious.

It seemed like a giant had taken a vacuum cleaner to the land. I had seen results of other tornadoes with my

Alabama Power days. They did not come close to this damage. Trees were not just broken, they were gone. The town was littered with wires, broken power poles, debris from buildings and everything you can imagine. We tried to drive South and could not drive less than a half mile. There were zero landmarks. Houses, barns, trailers, old stores were just gone. I grew up in this area and I could not tell where I was.

I distinctly remember as we came North into town there was a tractor trailer with a load of lumber headed South. Now we were going South, I saw the same truck. However, it was facing North, with not a piece of lumber on the trailer. I heard later the driver survived, however 18 people did not.

The real problem was I could see where our house used to be. I should not have been able to see if there were still trees. Sherry looked at me and we were in too much shock to cry. We were just numb. I remember Sherry asking, “what do we do now?” I replied, “let’s try to help someone else.

We stop where some people were searching a home site. We looked and called for them. We were unable to find the young man. He was later found alive about 100 yards from where we looked. As we drove toward what was the town I looked to my left. There stood a cow just leisurely eating grass.

I looked at the school and saw it had collapsed. Mr. Hollingsworth, Marion County School Superintendent, saved countless lives by canceling school for the day. There were two houses and a store in the middle of the path, damaged but still standing. Everything around them was destroyed. The other observation was the water tower was still standing. Hackleburg was also struck in 1943 by a tornado, that same water toward withstood that storm.

Bitter or Better; it is your choice

Sherry is a nurse, so we went to Hackleburg First Baptist church which had become a drop-off point. I am immensely proud of what happened next. We had lost everything, but I watched Sherry start treating and caring for injured people. It was so hectic that I started helping with triage. In the parking lot we were trying to get the seriously injured into the local flower shop van to take to hospital.

The reaction of Hackleburg people was so wonderful to see. With the path and destruction of tornado, the roads were blocked from help coming into town. When the team from Florence hospital was able to get into town, there was nothing for them to do. The Rescue Squad, Hackleburg Volunteer Fire Department, Street Department, Police Department and basically everyone physically able, just went to work to help their neighbors.

Bitter or Better; it is your choice

Then I heard Rob's mother screaming in pain and wanting to know about her husband. I ran over and got her attention and grabbed her hand. She immediately calmed down and thanked me for being there. I told her he was inside and being treated by medics. I told her she had to get to the hospital. I would make sure her husband knew she was okay. I know God had me there at that place, at that time.

The other image that sticks in my mind was this young woman who got out of a car and walked up to the church. She was walking on the outside of her right ankle. She did not even know the difference. She sat down and told me, "I really need a cigarette." I found her one and lit it for her. I said, "ma'am please do not look down, but your right foot is broken." She had this blank stare on her face and said, "it is".

Bitter or Better; it is your choice

I drove the three miles west to the community of Wiginton to check on my parents. Their power was out, and they had no clue what had happened. I told them, “Hackleburg is gone, and Sherry and I have lost everything.

An enormously powerful EF5 tornado had destroyed Hackleburg. Sherry and I would find out all we had were the clothes on our back. If you are holding on to some earthly object you need to let it go. Trust me when I tell you it can all be gone in 30 seconds. However, God was once again about to show his Power.

We stayed with my parents that night and tried to drive to our house the next morning. There were National Guard checkpoints set up to prevent sightseers. I told the man that my house was just up the next hill. His look confirmed what I already knew. I said I know it’s gone, but my wife, daughter and I just need to see if we can salvage anything. He said , "follow that State Trooper."

<u>Bitter or Better; it is your choice</u>

We drove around a curve and started up the hill, everything changed. Sherry's uncle's house was destroyed but they survived. Her cousins' trailer was destroyed, she did not survive. This tornado was estimated to have winds of 210 mph and stayed on the ground an amazing 132 miles. The storm had intensified and merged with another system quite literally over their house.

Bobby told me later that he was sitting at kitchen table when the roof vanished, and an inside door slammed into him. He and his wife held the door over themselves and their infant grandson. As they were getting up his wife stated, "there is another one coming." They barely made it to storm house and shut the door when it hit. Either a separate tornado or a fingerling from the massive storm struck first. As this one passed by, he knew his daughter was dead. He prayed that we had heeded the warning and were still alive.

Bitter or Better; it is your choice

I now looked up the hill where our home was, and there was nothing. As we drove up, I noticed bushes that used to be around our home, but there was nothing inside of them. There was nothing to salvage, it was all destroyed or just gone.

There are no true words to describe the emptiness that smothers you. We had Nothing! The sheer numbness is beyond words. We ended up just aimlessly walking around. My truck was in the edge of the woods about 100 yards away. I had a pistol in my go-bag behind the seat. The barrel was bent but was still in the backpack. A couple of days later my keys were found embedded in a tree.

Sherry's brother Josh and sisters Sheila and Charlotte with husband Jeff showed up to help. Ron and Sharon drove over to help. They searched a mass of pine trees for three days and did not find anything worth keeping. The force of the tornado had blown the pine trees in different directions. Simply moving fifteen feet was a labor-intensive effort.

There had been a folded lawn chair leaning against the house. It simply was blown over, while my pickup was three hundred feet away and our house ½ mile away. There was sod stripped off the ground leaving dirt spots. A guide wire is three strands of wire with each having seven strands. It is what secures a power pole in position. The guide wire in front yard was unraveled!

That afternoon my cell phone rang, it was Becky, and she was hot. "Mark and I have a pickup load of drinks, snacks and things for you, and I reckon this Trooper thinks we are just tricking him so we can come steal something." I had to calm her down while laughing and tell her another way to come to the house.

I was hoping it would be someone local that would allow her in. Thankfully, there was. In the back of the pickup was more than what she had said. There were purses for Sherry and Erin, ball caps, socks, jackets, clothing and then she handed the envelope. “That is to buy whatever you will need, she said. "Wow" is what I thought.

Over the course of my cancer fight I had collected a variety of Cross figurines and wall hangings. I mentioned to Ron that if only I could find one. He went back to the site and looked for about 4 hours. He found a piece from four different crosses. The pieces were all from different sides so together they form a cross. They hang in a shadowbox in my office.

On Thursday I saw what I was looking for. Those white Alabama Power pickups that I knew had the evaluators. When at major storm strikes, the area must be evaluated to decide what is needed. On Friday I saw the convoy of big trucks drive up Highway 43. I had been part of that convoy before and had looked at the blank faces. This time I understood the blank stares, Hope is Here!

Then an APCo truck drove up and out stepped my friend Corey, who oversaw the crews. He stepped out with his radio in his hand. "I have someone who wants to talk to you," he smiled. It was Danny Glover. He had to personally talk to me and find out what I needed. It was 7 years and 6 months since Hurricane Ivan.

Saturday was just more searching with no results. I sat down in the lawn chair and a group of about ten people drove up to help. I told them to go help someone that could salvage something. The despair hung on me. We had no house, no clothes, no household items, we had nothing. See how the narrative plays on my mind. Then I was reminded my family was alive and unharmed. The pity day was over.

Hackleburg started taking care of itself within hours. Supplies came in for those of us who lost everything.

Bitter or Better; it is your choice

A collection station was set up at the football field. Area churches had places for us to pick up items. FEMA did not show up till day SIX! A small community just does not have big priority when a major city is also struck. Things ran smoother without them!

The collection station was moved three times over the next several months. They even tried to close it down and move to a nearby city. I heard the police chief finally had to tell them nothing was leaving Hackleburg.

Sunday afternoon Sherry's Aunt Barbara called. Sherry tells me that Barbara and Gary want us to come to their house. My thought was, really? Yeah, sure, we aren't in the middle of anything. We drove up to their house and they were outside. Gary says y'all just follow me because there is someone, we want to introduce you too. The extra mile we drive I am thinking just how weird this is.

Bitter or Better; it is your choice

We stop and walk in where Gary introduces us to Bobby and Sue Bowen. We talk about ourselves a little. We tell them how we lost everything and are just trying to get traction to figure out where to start. Sue walks over and hands me the keys to the house. She says, “Well, me and Bobby want to help someone. Here are the keys and this house is now yours for as long as you need it. We are going to the lake.”

I look around the room and everyone has the biggest smile ever. I look at Sherry and she is in shock just like me. Bobby and Sue Bowen reflected Jesus Christ in that moment more than anyone I had ever met. We did not just get the use of a house, we gained two precious people in our lives. Those four months gave us a chance to decompress before making any decisions.

The back story is even an only Jesus moment. After the morning church service people were standing around talking. Barbara overheard Sue ask another woman if she knew anyone that had been affected by the tornado. Barbara said, "my Niece and her husband lost everything!" Sue told Barbara and Gary to bring us to the house so they could meet us. .

Then we started being loved on by the pastor Brother Jerome Sherrill. He would bring food and then a couple of times there was a check from Mt. Hebron Church. God gave me another sign because of all the churches and pastors; this pastor's son, Mike, worked at Alabama Power. I had known Mike for years.

Clint Knowles, pastor of Hackleburg of Church of God of Prophesy, stepped up to help us. Even though their church and parsonage were destroyed, he worked hard in the recovery efforts of Hackleburg. Pastor Clint would call me to stop by so he could give us gas cards other churches across the country had donated.

Bitter or Better; it is your choice

Since lost my truck I needed transportation. I put a note on social media. My friend Brad Alsup let me know he would let me drive his Jeep. I drove for months while fighting FEMA to reimburse for our losses. (I was turned down three times before approved) That small act was big in our ability to recover. The entire ruse of Government agencies is to decline, decline and decline just hoping you will give up.

Barbara and Mal drove up to just love on us. Several day later, Roger drove up to see me. We were at the house site and buttercups were blooming. He dug up several to take home and plant at his home in Birmingham. Every Spring he sends me a picture of them blooming. That picture is just a reassurance from God. No matter what life throws at me, I have a fresh beginning with Him.

The community continued to offer support. I discover storage tubs as the best item. As we went from site to site to gather donations, tubs became a way to store items. When a storm hits, I recommend you send help to Samaritans Purse, Salvation Army, or a church organization. Trust me when I tell you the agency you see on TV begging for help, does not help.

We lived in ‘our’ house and continued to be loved by Brother Jerome and the members of Mt. Hebron. One day I told Sherry that is the church we are attending when everything settles down. Gary and Barbara continued to do things for us. We decided to find a lot and buy a double wide trailer to move into. Gary talked to Denton and Della Ruth about a piece of property next door to them. The lot is owned by their son, James. He was okay with us to place our home there. There was no charge during the three plus years we lived there.

In August I am standing with Denton on the acre of land, meeting with man who is going to deliver our trailer the next day. He informs me that there needs to be gravel spread to make a pad for the trailer. I am freaking out however Denton tells me to call Vic Nix (who I had never met) to get the gravel. Vic tells me to call Chris Lynch (who I had never met) to bring me a load. Chris brings the gravel and Denton uses his tractor and rest of afternoon spreading it out so our home could be delivered the next morning.

We loved Denton and Della Ruth so much. He was Deacon at Mt. Hebron and one of the humblest men I have ever known. He was always doing and helping without wanting attention. Della Ruth became our Sunday School teacher. All these people showing Christ in their actions and deeds still humbles me. We joined Mt. Hebron.

In our desperate situation, God was handling everything. I could not even see a place to start. God was just merely reminding me, 'Stay with Me'.

Bitter or Better; it is your choice

More Opportunities

During 2010 we had found out mom had multiple melanoma. This is a horrible cancer with very slim survival odds. We prayed and mom fought. Sharon and I would take turns driving her to appointments. I was able to learn so about her in those weeks. I will cherish those talks forever.

Mom passed away before we could move into our new home. She had the determination (most people call it stubbornness) beyond most people. We were around her bed as she was struggling to breathe. I held her hand and leaned over. I said, "mom, it's okay, you can quit fighting and go on to Heaven."

In her semi unconscious state, I saw her frown. I said, "okay, do it your way." I promise you I saw a smirk on her face. She joined Heaven on August 9, 2011, one week shy of 75th birthday. I had the absolute honor and privilege to speak at her funeral.

Dad was fighting his own health issues. Plus, he was lost without his companion of 53 years. He never really found anything to keep busy. His health declined and he passed away December 3, 2012.

Dad left strict instructions that he was too be cremated and have no service. Mom would always mention a name and state, “They will not see me when I need to see them. But I bet they will be at my funeral!” They were! Dad saw this and stated he did not want people looking at me. "I needed to see them when I was alive."

I noticed this while mom was battling cancer. Do NOT avoid going to see someone that is having a major health problem. It is not about you not wanting to see them look so bad. Trust me when I say, we know how we look.

But we need to see you and visit. A visit or phone call is as good a medicine as there is.

When you visit, do not feel like you have to say anything. There are no magic words. Besides, it is hard to remember what was said. However, I can tell you every person who just simply showed up. Job had three of the best friends in the world, until they opened their mouths.

On February 7, 2013, Liam, our first grandchild, came into the world. I had lost so much within the past 22 months. God knew I would need Liam in the years still to come.

As we began the process of finding our new normal, my hips were worsening. Finally, I made appointment to see the surgeon. On July 23, 2013, I had the right hip replacement performed. I waited this time until I fully recovered. Then on December 2, 2014, the replacement of the left hip was completed.

<u>Bitter or Better; it is your choice</u>

To my pleasant surprise, the replacement operations were better that the resurfacing. Probably helped that I was doing them one at a time. The surgeries were a four-inch incision on the front of torso, instead of an eight-inch cut on the buttock area. There was not the amount of muscle and tendons cut. This time I also worked to get therapy before the surgery.

At this point Roger and Ron would ask me, "who did you see this time." On every trip there was someone placed in my path. Once it was the lab tech that drew my blood. It could be a patient in waiting room. It might be a nurse or doctor. The beauty of it was I never knew. I would pray God would give me the words for that person.

Each of us should be doing this. It is all about slowing down and being aware. I am not talking about buying a meal for a stranger, and then posting on social media so everyone knows. I mean put your phone down and let the Holy Spirit lead you. You do not have to give a sermon or have all the answers. You never know if you are sowing, or watering.

One of toughest and yet rewarding is when God led me to Randy. His son played football and baseball and I knew that his dad had been diagnosed with cancer. However, I did not how to break the ice and talk with him. Then in the Fall of 2012, I received a call from Randy sister-in-law. She told me he was struggling and would I reach out. I never told anyone until writing in this book.

Randy graduated high school seven years after me. However, I knew him, and I knew a lot of family. I called and asked if I could stop by and visit. The first time we talked our friendship just clicked. Using what Paul taught me, all I did was listen. When he would ask a question, I would answer but he just needed an ear.

Bitter or Better; it is your choice

I started going by more often and we told stories or talked sports as much as anything. Over the course of a couple of years we just talked. He told me one day that he could tell me stuff and I did not judge him. There are deep and somewhat dark things that prey on your mind when you battle cancer. I had experienced every thought that Randy did. This helped him and me. We always held hands and prayed before I left. I just talked with God and prayed for Comfort in the house.

The class of 1985 impressed me with the love they showered on Randy. There was an annual golf tournament with all proceeds going to Randy and family. He told me after the 2014 tournament that he did not understand why they did this for him. I was able to tell him it was simply payback. I reminded him of the story of you reap what you sow. I told him he had sowed good seed all his life and this allowed people to show him how much it had meant to them.

The last time I saw Randy was in his hospital bed. Family and friends were all there. When I walked in, his other son Micah just bear hugged me for couple of minutes. I whispered in his ear that the suffering would be over soon. I went to his bedside and there were no words, just our eyes telling each other how we felt.

Then our friend James asked me if I would pray. I thanked God for the example Randy had shown and the influence he had on people. I then asked for Mercy and for the suffering to end. When I leaned over Randy mouthed 'thanks'. I hugged his sweet wife Tina and told her it would not be much longer. I then realized that Andrew was not there yet. Randy passed away shorty after Andrew arrived.

In April 2015 God opened a permanent door for us to stay in Spruce Pine. After 3 years it was time to find a house if possible. Again, we mentioned to Barbara and Gary. Two days later Gary had a lead for us. A gentleman down the road from them had his house and acreage for sale just the year before. He told Gary it was for sale.

Two days later we are walking around the home and the owner quoted a price. I accepted it on the spot. I knew this made him nervous, but I assured him later it was close to the appraised price. Chris (who brought the gravel) is now my neighbor and friend. I have no way of to do upkeep on the land. His oldest son, Sam, raises cattle on and maintains the pasture. His other son Sawyer is always helping me.

Within four years we had went from losing everything we owned in a tornado, to owning a home with property. Bro Ray Edgar was once my pastor of the church I attended as a teenager. His son, David, is now my

neighbor. There are no coincidences, God is always confirming.

Bitter or Better; it is your choice

Consequences

Our second grandson, Rhett, was born in May 2016. We continued to settle in our home. Sherry and I both had a serious issue of forgetfulness. We would start to look for something and then it would hit us, tornado. We lost all our family photos. Sherry would sometime tell me that if I would have told her what I saw, she would have run in and grabbed stuff. I said, "yep, and we would be buried somewhere today."

During my cancer and chemotherapy, I had no taste. I ate because I knew I had too. You could give a piece of meat, a vegetable or a piece of cardboard and they would have all tasted the same. On more than one occasion I proclaimed that when I got well, that I would eat all I want, whenever I wanted it. I did exactly that.

With my poor decisions, weakened immune system and history of heart disease in my family; it was all just a matter of time. That time came on the afternoon of September 27, 2016.

I was in CVS Russellville, Alabama and suddenly I broke out in a sweat and felt nauseous. I checked out and made it my vehicle. All the sudden I had indigestion. Instead of calling for help I headed home. While still about a mile from the house I knew I was in trouble. My jaws started hurting. At this point I was praying to God that I would not hurt anyone when I wrecked.

I made it inside the house when a pain hit my chest that brought me to my knees. I took a couple of baby aspirin and called... Sherry at work! I told her I loved her, and I was quite sure I was having a heart attack. I had googled it and I had 9 of the 12 symptoms. She said, "call 911 and I am calling Barbara and Gary."

I called 911, took another baby aspirin and laid down on the couch. Why did I call Sherry first? Of everything I had been through I thought this was the one. My jaws almost locked up, I could only take short breaths, my shoulder blades were pulling forward and it felt like a butcher knife was now in my chest.

Barbara and Gary arrived first. Gary said later that I had no color and knew I was in trouble. As they rolled me to ambulance, I gave my keys to Gary. I looked and there was Sawyer, and he did not know what to think. I asked him to take care of our dog. Jack.

When I arrived at Russellville Hospital ER, Sherry was there waiting. Pastor Scott and his wife Jeannie, Barbara and Gary thankfully were there for her. The staff did a great job stabilizing me, but a problem came up. There were no helicopters available so I would have to be put back in Ambulance for 30-minute ride to ECM Hospital in Florence.

They started rolling me out and I stopped them. I told them I wanted my pastor to pray. Brother Scott told me later that everyone heard me! They told me how we had to move. I told them we were not leaving till the prayer. I knew we needed protected. When he finished, I was loaded, and Sherry jumped in the passenger seat.

While traveling north on Highway 43, I could see familiar landmarks zipping by. The paramedic and I were chatting as we traveled. Suddenly she stopped talking as she looked at EKG. Then she told the driver, "Tell them we are going straight to the Cath lab and not the ER." I asked was there something on the printout she did not like. She replied, "Mr. Hood, you are having a major heart attack, right now! "She popped two more nitroglycerin pills under my tongue and the ambulance sped up.

Jason and I have our own inside joke. One day we talked about all the things I have gone through. We wondered aloud, what would finally kill me. I thought to myself, Jason we are about to find out.

In that moment, the Peace and Comfort of Jesus filled me. I knew someone else was in the back of that ambulance. I could sense someone in the corner looking at me. I remember thinking, "are you here to get me?" "No, I am here to Comfort. You will not die. Liam will need you,"

Chills have run over my body just typing those words. When we stopped and they pulled me out. I looked at Sherry and told her, "I am not going to die. Don't worry I will not die. Liam is going to need me." I notice Sharon standing there with the four that had been in Russellville. They rushed me straight to the Cath lab.

I want to try to explain what being close to death is like. It is satan final attempt to sway and attack. The physical pain was not the issue, it was the phycological games. I was reminded of everything that had happened and how would a God that loved me let me go through that? I was reminded of little things I regretted during my life. I have had to audibly tell satan to shut up.

I had gotten there so quick, there were not set up yet. Dr Lango and the technicians were asking me questions while they are hooking me up to monitors. They were changing into scrubs, fixing the table, supplies and doing evaluation on me in an organized chaos. They started to shave me, and I ask them, "I am going to be put to sleep?" I at least got a chuckle from them. Dr Lango said, "yes, right about now."

This event triggered another downward spiral. I woke to find out I had two stints. I had survived what is known as the 'widow maker'. This was the fourth time God had decided it wasn't time for me to come Home.

The next day Sharon and Dre came for a visit Walked a little bit with him and just talked. I was amazed at how I could breathe and not get tired. I had to be careful, but Jack and I were walking soon after.

The heart attack had severely damaged the left side of my heart. I had bi-weekly appointments with Dr. Lango and was taking part in Cardiac Rehab. I felt good again but after several months the fatigue kept getting worse. I reached the point that I would be talking to someone, and dose off. Therefore, I stopped driving at this point. This even causes depression to creep in.

God had placed another friend in my life, Hubert Chance. Hubert was forced to retire at age 55 due to heart problems. I spoke to him at church and liked him because he was as upfront as I was when he talked. A member of our church passed away and his wife was there. I asked about Hubert, and she said that he did not do funerals very well.

Bitter or Better; it is your choice

I had gone to church with the man for several years but did not know the tragedy they had experienced. The Lord led me to go visit him. He builds birdhouses in the Fall and Winter. As a carpenter he did this to keep busy. I dropped in one day at his shop and we talked, but mostly I listened. Hubert and I discovered we needed each other.

Bitter or Better; it is your choice

Mission Field

When I started feeling worse, Hubert is one that pushed me to get another opinion. His words were more like, “they are going to let you die”. Since everything else was at UAB, I asked my Internal Medicine doctor to make me an appointment with Cardiology. It was now mid-2017 and another testimony was coming.

I was now under the care of Doctor Chapman at UAB. He believes I had another episode or event in July 2017 which caused my heart to decrease output. I needed to have a Nuclear Stress test. Sherry and I went, I had the test, and we were waiting on results and planning lunch. We were called back, and a doctor came in and went over the results and I understood my heart was not in good shape. Then the aide came in and set down. She looked at Sherry and said, “I am so sorry.”

Bitter or Better; it is your choice

I am sitting right next to Sherry, but she did not tell me she was sorry. She said another doctor needed to review and we could just wait where we were. I looked at Sherry and knew this was not good. Then Dr. Chapman came and told me I was being admitted. All sorts of tests were completed and then I was told my heart was only in the 20% range. The top of the range is 75% so I was not critical, yet. I was told my heart was dying. There would be many serious decisions in my future.

During this time, we were being told about VAD's and the Transplant Team. On one of appointments, I noticed a man with the batteries with an empty chair next to him. I sat down and asked about how it worked. I had met a new friend, Frankie. For about 30 minutes he told me everything. He explained the VAD, he discussed how the clinic worked, and told me in detail about every member of the Team. I felt like I knew everyone from his conversation. Then he said something that I repeat to other when I talk to them, "We are a Family, everyone is here to help."

In August 2017 a Cardioverter Defibrillator was implanted to kick start the heart in case it stopped or got out of rhythm. During this time the Heart Transplant Team began watching my case. In February 2018, I was admitted because my ejection factor was now in the teens. I was admitted to the Heart and Lung Transplant ICU or HTICU.

I was in HTICU for a week this time. Every test related to the heart was ran on me. If it was uncomfortable, I would start up the choir in my head and pray for the person doing test. This time something was different. A different transplant doctor came in each day. Every Coordinator and nurse stuck their head in at some point.

They performed every test you can think of. A lung test where I had to do all the blowing tests into a machine.

<u>Bitter or Better; it is your choice</u>

One test was a 4D of my chest cavity, so they got exact measurements of space. At one point, I quit wondering about what they were doing; I would set there and think, "Who thought this up."

Then it hit me, we were being evaluated. Every person had input on whether I qualified for possible transplant. They were not going to make a mistake. When dealing with the gift of an organ you cannot make a mistake. We even had the social worker and the business office make a visit. Because you must be financially able, mentally capable, and physically strong enough to endure. They were also noticing Sherry and I interaction.

Transplant is a lifetime commitment. I must take anti-rejection medicines for the rest of my life. Then there are medicines to protect your body from the anti-rejection medicines. They are continually checked and adjusted.

These medicines are not cheap; therefore, you must show you can afford them.

Yen and Lauren were the main two people I saw at this point. I found out later that the Team checked with my other doctors. I was told that Dr. Forero had played a big influence in me being accepted. All those times of doing exactly what he told me had now come full circle. The Team had a firsthand witness on my behavior and ability to follow instructions.

I was accepted in the Heart Transplant program and was now fully under their supervision. Yet another God event had occurred. Dr Forero left UAB in July of 2018, barely 3 months after my acceptance. I wonder if I would have been accepted if he had already left? Even I realize that I was not a top-notch candidate.

In May 2018 I was admitted to HTICU and had a balloon pump inserted in the artery behind my aorta. This pump would inflate and deflate to push the blood through my system. I laid flat for 7 days. I could only raise the head of bed 15 degrees. That is about one pillow.

On the seventh day the surgeon Dr. Hoopes came in and said we could not wait any longer. My ejection factor was below 10% and we had to act. I signed three sets of paperwork. 1) if the heart was too damaged then they would close me with no action, 2) implant a Left Ventricular Assist Device or 3) if a heart became available, I would have the transplant.

I remember thinking I should be stressed, but I was not. I told Sherry where the insurance documents were and talked with Jesus all night. This would be the fifth time I approached death. After surgery June 5, 2018, I woke in CICU with a LVAD. I also woke in a full-blown, 5 alarm panic attack.

Bitter or Better; it is your choice

I woke with monitors beeping all around the room. I had tubes sticking out of me everywhere it seemed. The pain in my chest was searing through my body. I saw about eight people but none of them was Sherry. I freaked out is the best I can put it.

I started asking, "where I was? "What had they done with Sherry?" "Why did I have all these tubes?" "Had Sherry just dumped me here." The strange thing was my brain was trying to tell my mouth to shut up, but my mouth was not listening! My brain knew all the answers, but my mouth kept spouting off.

They were having to hold me down to keep me from hurting myself. Then a nurse got in my face and was telling me to calm down. “Your wife has been here the entire time. She just left for a little bit to walk your grandchildren to the car.” My mouth listened to him!

Bitter or Better; it is your choice

As I laid there still agitated, another nurse walked over to give me a message from the next cubicle. I say cubicle but the entire CICU is nothing but curtains. They must be able to move quickly if someone gets in trouble. The message was, "I am praying for you, everything will be okay." God had an Angel right next door for me! I became suddenly calm.

The pain while in CICU was never really controlled. I had been on pain medicine for 14 years, so my body did not react to what I was receiving. I also learned to hate the sound of the portable x-ray machine. A cold, hard, eighteen square inch thing had to be placed under me. This was done to ensure all was well inside my chest. Later, I could hear that thing coming and just hope it was not for me.

Physical Therapy came by in the morning. It was time to get up. For about 10 minutes we worked to get me up. Scoot to edge of chair, use your legs and not your arms to push up, IV lines it seemed everywhere. I finally get up with 5 nurses encouraging and helping.

As we start our walk, Sherry pushes the recliner behind us, just in case. I took the hardest seven steps I have ever taken in my life. I had laid on my back for eight days, so my muscles were gone. I sit down and am just despondent I could not do any more. The nurses are praising me but inside I am having doubts.

Bitter or Better; it is your choice

LVAD

This is open heart surgery. Instead of repairing or replacing the heart, an electric pump was pushed into the bottom of heart. A control line is run out through the abdomen to a control panel (I called this my Xbox controller). Everything ran off the batteries that now had to be worn. I used a fly-fishing vest with a battery in each pouch and the controller had a pocket. I tried a football girdle pad with batteries in thigh pad area and controller in the jock strap slot. I was worried about bathing, but we figured out a to cover drive line area and take a shower.

I want to explain what happens when you lay flat on your back for eight days. You get constipated and bed sores. Now in CICU you do not lay in bed all day. As soon as I was awake, the nurses got me out of bed, and I sat in a recliner. The bed is pushed off to the side just in case you get any ideas.

I was hurting from bed sores, so the cream was applied several times a day. This and getting me up to walk ensured I was moving around. On June 7th I was asked when my last bowel movement was. What came next was not pleasant in any way. Since I could not lay down, I was cleaned out while standing over a plastic sheet. I told them at one point they would be scratching my throat very soon. Again, it is best to bring some laughter to things if you can.

They allowed Liam, Rhett, and Erin came to visit me for small periods of time. Just seeing my boys lifted my spirits. I found that when I am bedridden or very sick, I need these memories. When I would feel bad, I would play my memories.

I was moved to the HTICU recover. One of the conditions to discharge is walking a mile, in one day. That does not sound like much, until ever step is labor intensive. I told Sherry after one walk that I had made a serious mistake.

Then the door next to me would fly open and out came this man pushing an IV pole with the Auburn mascot on top. He just walked, constantly, just walked. Due to HIPPA the nurses cannot divulge information about another patient. However, they can let the other person know you would like to talk.

This wonderful man had not been out of the hospital in two years. His immune system had somehow developed antibodies against organ coming from the Southeast. This man was a role model for me. If I ask, he would tell me everything. The inspiration for me was watching his actions. He never complained or seemed upset. He walked and walked and walked.

Then I met Jim Murrell. He had received a heart transplant in 2013 and was an encyclopedia of knowledge. He simply stepped in the room and introduced himself and asked if I had any questions. Of course, I did, and we had a nice conversation. This was just the start of a friendship. He has a YouTube channel "The Transplant Helper." I highly encourage looking through his calendar for a topic that will help you.

This is major lifestyle adjustment. Sherry and I had to be trained how to change the batteries and well and disconnecting and connecting to base unit that was plugged into wall for bed. The drive line site must be kept clean and dry. We had to stay in Birmingham for two weeks post LVAD. This was to ensure everything was okay before we traveled too far from the hospital.

I was not very nice to Sherry or anyone the first couple of days. I was sure the drive line or one the drain tubes in my chest would be pulled. This was because of a bad experience. During the cancer hospital stays I always had a catheter. One day the tubing caught in the items in my nurses pocket. She turned to walk away, I was coming out of the bed screaming; stop! stop! After that I always kept excess IV tubing looped around my hand. I also kept close watch on anyone near my bed

When discharged we stayed at a local hotel. Then we were blessed and humbled by Mike and Gail from Demopolis. The snacks and drinks were wonderful, but something deeper touched me. These were friends I worked with Youth in church years before. Later that Summer, Mike and David drove four hours with all lawn equipment. They mowed and trimmed the entire area around our pond.

When I came home, I had to notify the nearest organized Fire Department. I had to have three other people that knew the procedure of my LVAD and know where I always was. While I was in HTICU, I named my LVAD George, after Hugo the Abominable Snowman in Bugs Bunny. *I will hold him, I will hug him, I will love him, and I will call him George.*

The paperwork signed for LVAD states patient will use the VAD until transplant or end of life. The huge benefit is it keeps you alive. The only negative is you come off the Transplant Waiting List until it is decided you can withstand the necessary surgery.

It is amazing how wearing oversized batteries can become a witnessing tool. I continued to be as active as I could. I went to Liam flag football games. People would of course ask what they were, which gave me a change to give a quick testimony. I stayed active with Cardiac Rehab.

Sherry and I (and George) loaded my base unit and attended the National Quartet Convention in Gatlinburg TN that Fall. Since the later was out of State the area hospital was notified when we would be there. Also, I live two-hours from UAB, so my instructions were to get to nearest ER. I was to let them stabilize me only, call UAB and they would come get me.

While attending the Convention I was able to personally thank Jason Crabb of the Crabb Family. I know he may hear from thousands of people, but I wanted him to know how God had used Through the Fire. When I shook his hand, I thanked him for all their music and told him I was running off batteries. When what I said registered with him, he took a step back like 'wow. He then placed his hand over my heart and prayed that I would receive my heart.

The corridors are packed with people and activities. I started to sit down on a bench and the woman said she was expecting someone. I said I was sorry, but I just needed to catch my breath and check my batteries on my heart. She of course told me to sit and was intrigued. She said the bench was her witness bench because her husband helped in the vending area. For 20 minutes we talked and shared our Faith. She was calling people over to tell them my story. I believe God received full use of the witness bench.

On November 1, 2018, I had appointments most of the day at the Kirklin Clinic Included were the VAD clinic, Wound Care to ensure the bed sores were healed and a follow-up with Patient Services. Later I received notice that I had been placed back on the transplant list effective November 12, 2018. God once again was about to remind me, "I got this".

Bitter or Better; it is your choice

New Life

Friday, November 16th I was not feeling well. Sherry was at work, and I just laid around the house. Elsewhere, a tragedy had occurred that directly affected me, but I did not know it yet.

Saturday I still wasn't feeling well and had a temperature. I called the on-call desk and told them I had a fever of 101.3. In a few minutes I received a call from Stephanie, the on-call Coordinator. I explained what happened and again said I had a fever of 101.3. I was told to head to Birmingham and to come straight to the HTICU. I found out later that BOTH people, separate from each other, had wrote fever as 103.1!

I was admitted, checked out thoroughly with lab and blood cultures were taken. My fever was now only 99.1 but actions were still being taken on the incorrect 103.1. I was bored so I began walking the halls. Taking the que that Jim had shown I would stop and talk if someone gave the sign they wanted too.

There was another patient walking toward me, and I literally saw a glow around him. I stopped to talk and my friendship with Bennie officially began. He was waiting for LVAD and was having some minor issues. Late that evening they decided I could go home but before discharge I said my goodbyes to Bennie and his wife Tonya.

Sherry drove the two hours home and we unloaded the vehicle. I took a shower and laid down for the night. It was now about 11:00 PM. Within 15 minutes my cell phone rang and a nurse from HTICU called. She told me that the doctors wanted me to return to the hospital. I foolishly said we were tired, and would it be okay if we just came back in the morning? In less than two minutes the phone rang again. It was Stephanie and her words were a little more direct. "Mr. Hood," she said, "It is your decision to wait or not. However, a bed is being prepared for you right now." Maybe it was the way she said – right now- but I told her we would load up and head that way.

We arrived back and I was admitted around 1:00 AM, Sunday the 18th. The blood culture had come back, and I was started on IV antibiotic. After breakfast I started walking. I walked with Bennie, chatted with nurses, and a couple of patients. One will always stay with me. As you walk around the corridor you can tell if someone feels like chatting. The door being wide open and eye contact is a 'yes'.

I could see this man had all his bags ready and was waiting on transport. I said, "looks like you get to go home". He looked at me and said," I am going home to die, I am too sick to be a candidate." At that moment time stopped and Jesus took over. I found myself sitting beside his bed and asking if I could pray with him. I prayed for him and his family. thanked Jesus for his testimony and for comfort for the days ahead. He then prayed and his words ring in my head, "Lord thank you for this man and I ask You to give this man a new heart." I walk to my room and cry; it takes a few minutes before I can explain to Sherry.

Around 2:00 PM on the 18th, the surgeon, Dr. Hoopes stuck his head in the door. I was sitting in the side chair and his comment means more now that when I first heard it, "oh, you are not in bed", I said, "no sir I have been walking." He listens to my lungs and then has me turn my head as far to the left, then right and then down to my chest as I can. He does not say much, I get bored, so I walk some more. Do you get the picture that walking is important?

Around 3:30 the weekend Transplant team physician comes into my room. Dr. Jolly said it is one of the strangest reactions she has ever had. I am sitting in the chair and Sherry is sitting on the bed beside me. Dr. Jolly starts, “Well we have some news” (my brain thinks okay, we know what the infection is, and they are going to discharge me), “we think we have a heart for you.” I turn to Sherry to see if she heard what I did. I turn back to Dr. Jolly and said, “would you repeat that.” She tells me again and I believe I did a fist pump and then hug Sherry.

What I now know is that a friend of my donor had saved my live. In a waiting room only a few hours earlier the family and friends were being told there was no hope. A nurse asked if he was a donor, his driver license was at the accident scene, and she spoke up ‘he is”. No one else knew that he was.

Things spend up now and I am signing paperwork and being prepped for surgery. This is about to happen! Dr. Hoopes steps in and goes over the details of the operation. He explained that until the organ is at UAB he does not know if it will be a match. Then I am asked a strange question, “do you wish to proceed?” I said of course, a thousand times yes! Do people ever say no? You would be surprised I am told.

The heart is from a young man. Ordinarily it would not work for me. However, my other organs had adapted to the poor oxygen and blood flow. The LVAD was keeping me alive. Dr. Hoopes explained that my organs were smaller and would develop back as this heart grew. Every case is different, and in my case, I had to be sick, but not too sick.

About 4 AM on the 19th I was under Spiritual attack. I mean intense, nonstop, attack straight from Hell. As I stated earlier, near death is the last hurrah for satan. It is last big effort to get me to curse or blame God. For about an hour all I could say, or think was, ‘Jesus’. Finally, I verbally got out, "Satan you are a liar now leave me alone."

<u>Bitter or Better; it is your choice</u>

Within 15 minutes the door opened, and it was Go time. The heart was a match! The infection was clear! The heart would fit in my chest cavity! I signed more paperwork and again was asked, “do you wish to proceed?” Absolutely I did so I said, let’s do it. I remember this trip so vividly. I kissed Sherry, told her where all the important documents were and told her, “I will see you when I wake up or when you get to Heaven."

The nurses were all smiling and telling me they would see me in a few days. As I was rolled down corridor after corridor I started to pray. I prayed for the surgeon, the operating room staff, Sherry, our children, grandchildren, each family member and their family, each friend and their family, and the granddaughter that was expected in December. I said a prayer for my donor's family,

There was no fear. Because I knew I would wake on earth with a new heart or in Heaven with a new body. I told the nurses with me I was praying for them. With the LVAD surgery, I was put to sleep in the hallway just before going into operating room. A doctor stepped out to deactivate my Defib device. I was moved into the operating room and helped get over on the table. I said, "I have been praying for all of you." Someone said, "thanks, we need them." Then I was out.

Bitter or Better; it is your choice

Day One of the Rest of my life

I woke about 5:30 PM on November 20, 2021. I was in surgery for about 10 hours. I was then in an induced coma with my chest packed with gauze. They do not close the chest until they see the heart is working and with no leaks or complications, or about 24 hours. Then I was slowly brought back to consciousness.

I woke to beeps and buzzers but thank God there was no panic attack. I slowly looked around and quickly realized that this was not Heaven. I saw Sherry in the corner and gave her the sign for I Love You. She walked over and I did it again. Her reply, "hook'em horns?" I became agitated and the nurse told me to wait a moment. He pulled the wires out of my throat (FYI, explains why they want to know how far you can turn your neck) He asked me if I remembered anything, and I told him no. He said, "good that means I did my job."

I whispered to Sherry, “I love you.” Once again it seems I have tubes everywhere. The nurse says they will move into the recliner in a few minutes. As I lay still, I felt it for the first time. The LVAD sounds like a washing machine vibrating in your head. Now I felt, thump-thump, thump-thump, thump-thump. I thanked God and I cried.

One month after my transplant, our 3rd grandchild was born, Bo Blake. It would be February before I could see her. I thank God often that there will some memory of me with my grand’s.

I was gotten up and moved to a recliner. You do not lie around in CICU. The same routine as LVAD, I need to walk to be ready to move to HTICU. Liam came for a visit on Wednesday. He had my cell phone telling me all the football scores. I walked every couple of hours, pushing past my earlier mark each time. I was expecting to me moved on Friday, but the nurses told me I may be there through the weekend.

I truly believe PTSD was triggered with thinking I would be there two more days. My panic attack came to my mind. I wanted to scream with all the beeping and noises going off. Then there were all the patients waking up from surgery. With everyone moaning and crying out, I could feel myself creeping toward going crazy.

I will forever be grateful to Dr. Jolly for what she did next. She came by about 6:00 PM and I begged and pleaded for her to get me out of CICU. She told me she would see what she could do. My spirits went lower as every 30-minute update from nurses was, no room available. At 9 PM the nurses told me housekeeping had been called in, but that if an emergency was admitted they would probably get the room.

I prayed and prayed while the doubt in my mind grew deeper. I felt like a time bomb inside. At 10:30 PM escort came to transport me to my room. I do not know what Dr. Jolly did, but she was an angel that night. I have been in hospital quite a bit. I never knew about anyone being discharged or rooms changed on Friday evening.

I was home again in HTICU, in my opinion the best group of nurses ever. On Saturday morning I started the activity I knew I would need to be discharged, I walked. Bennie was having issues with being able to receive a VAD. I stopped by his room and prayed with him. I encouraged him to walk with me. The following week he did have a LVAD implanted. For three weeks I walked, rested. Visited and then repeated them all again.

Tonya thanked me for encouraging Bennie. I saw as Frankie had told me; we are all a family. The halls of the corridor are a figure eight, with nurses' station at the four corners. You cannot walk outside the unit. Therefore, it gets sort of boring. I would walk one hallway back and forth, a big circle, figure eight; anything to break it up. I would walk early or later at night if possible. Less traffic just made it easier.

One morning my suspicions were confirmed. As I rounded the corner the nurse ask what lap that was. I think I said ‘five’ and her reply was “yes, you are right.” I knew they were counting too. The floor is very respectful to other patients.

One afternoon there was a lot of visitors around a room. I knew a family was about to face heartbreak. Everyone just walked the other side or did not walk to give family sort of privacy. No one had to tell us, we just all understand how close that situation is.

During my LVAD stay I had met Mamie, from housekeeping. She was in her late 60’s, but she outworked the rest of them. Sherry and I would just enjoy visiting with her. One day she was humming, and I ask if she sang in the choir. She snaped back, “why, you a preacher?” She Blessed me one day by signing “It Is Well”. She sang the words and not the song. I though what a shame that we will rush through verses instead of letting the words be a ministry.

I would have to stay within 20 minutes of the hospital upon discharge. I would have to walk my mile and be cleared by physician. Red Mountain Grace is a non-profit organization which leases apartments to people, like me, that need affordable temporary housing. The charge is $10 per night. Becky and Mark paid us for a month.

I want to add an observation from my many hospitals stays. Do not push the doctor and things will go better. Dr. Tallaj is head of the Transplant team. He is a wonderful doctor and has a wicked sense of humor. On

December 7 he made rounds and he thought everything looked good for me to go to the apartment.

He said one important word as he talked, *however*. I stopped him and told him if he wanted me to stay in hospital for the weekend, I was fine. I trust him and know he was in charge. He smiled and said, “I like that.” The nurse practitioner came back by to tell me I had made good points. Most everyone else was pushing to be discharged and it was refreshing for me to trust them.

The HTICU of UAB has the best teamwork I have seen. For first several days someone had to walk with me. The perfect example was I walked by a room and patient said something to nurse. Before he could turn to ask someone at the desk; they were already up and saying they had it. No one had just their duties, they all shared the care of patients.

Bitter or Better; it is your choice

On about the 10th day, I was walking the hall and I just stopped. My nurses wanted to know if I was ok. I said, "it just hit me, all the spare parts are gone." The arteries and veins come with the transplant. I celebrated no more coumadin. On discharge there is the ringing of the bell ceremony. The memory that stays the most is seeing my inspiration standing there, once again celebrating someone else.

My heart was about to be invigorated by riding in a car on the streets of Birmingham. Bennie was discharged that week and we ended up at the same apartment complex. Red Mountain is a wonderful group and truly stands for Christ. The apartments are furnished, and you are just expected to leave it stocked when you leave. The greatest thing was I could have visitors, Sherry could get a break and go home, and I could get outside to walk. Of course, someone had to stay with me. I was a mask wearer before it was cool to be a mask wearer!

Bitter or Better; it is your choice

Roger, Jason, Jerry, Ron, Sharon all plugged in days so Sherry could get a break. Dana and Aunt Joan brought me some homemade chicken and dumplings. On Christmas Eve a group from Red Mountain Ministries came with gifts and did some caroling. I was still going into clinic once a week for heart Cath and did physical therapy at Spain Rehab three times a week.

I was walking even while in the apartment. It was 16 steps from front door to back wall. I walked a mile every day even confined in the apartment. On nicer days I would walk the sidewalks around the apartments. So don't make excuses. Those that make excuses wonder why those that do not seem too to be able to rise above situations.

You must adapt to a new way of doing daily affairs. You must respect the donor. By doing that you will not go back to any old habits. Be ready to take pills, every day, for the rest of your life. That is a small thing to do for this gift.

Bitter or Better; it is your choice

Also, the medicine you must take are expensive. This is a fact for the rest of my life. There are organizations that will help you. In 2019, Becky led the effort for donations. Friends and family continue to Bless me. It is odd when you have no co-pay for medicines by the time September arrives.

Bitter or Better; it is your choice

My Hero

Cory Thigpen saved my life. Most everyone wants to know if I have been in contact with my donor family. With their okay and support I want to tell you about him. The phrase I heard often from his friends and family, "you got a good heart." They did not mean just physical good, but that he was a good soul and a good man.

Cory was on a road he often traveled. Exiting via the ramp when his car left the pavement. This caused him to lose control of his car. This happened on the Friday morning I was not feeling well and was told to come to HTICU.

On the Saturday I walked in HTICU; Cory was fighting for his life. He had so many friends at the hospital the group was moved to their own waiting area. I was told the hospital asked some to leave, they were answered by a very strong NO.

Bitter or Better; it is your choice

The people in the waiting area were some so many different backgrounds that many did not know each other. Cory was very active in Brazilian Jiu Jitsu. Basically, the entire dojo was there.

He was a bartender in the area and many people were there. He loved to skateboard, and those friends had to be there. Of course, his family was there praying for him to recover. The family had lost Cory's mother and grandmother within the past 12 months. Now they had to face this.

His friends told me he could talk about any music genre. For that matter he was well versed in any topic. Over and over, I heard how he always helped others. He would do without so he could help others.

He loved life and had a wonderful personality. I can visualize people being drawn to Cory by his love and caring. Most of all I see myself laughing at his jokes and really liking the man.

When Cory was 18, he had checked the box on his driver's license to be a donor. No one in his family knew. Most all his friends did not know; but there was one! His license was at the accident scene.

The family was notified that end of life seemed to be the result. So, on this Saturday afternoon a nurse asked the group, Is he a Donor? His friend spoke up and said, “yes”.

That put the hospital in motion. They checked the national registry and found he was a donor. UAB hospital was notified. The time fits when I was told to come back to the hospital after my discharge.

The misconception that needs to be addressed is, being a donor does not quicken the end of life. The donor is flown to Birmingham where the body is respectfully unhooked from life support. Then the various teams perform their duties. Great care is taken so the body is supported to lead to successful transplantation. All avenues of recovery are looked for before the decision is made.

On the Sunday afternoon I was told, “we may have a heart”; Cory was on his way to UAB. That is why it was Monday morning before the team was sure this heart would fit my chest cavity.

With the timetable and order of occurrences, I was not meant to get any heart. I know I was ordained to get Cory’s heart. Since my organs had reduced output so much, I needed a smaller heart. One that would grow and mature as my other organs responded.

After six months I was encouraged to write a letter to the family through Alabama Legacy of Hope. The letters are screened before mailing to the donor family. I was educated that not every family will respond. As a recipient we must be respectful of their decision. I exchanged several letters, but I told Sherry I needed to close the circle.

With the internet and basic information, I was able to figure out who my donor was and where he was from. I did not break protocol to meet the family. After my January 2020 follow up, we were packed and ready for the trip.

My decision was to drop by the Jiu-Jitsu facility. I walked into the gym and was very unsure of how I would be received. What I saw was a true show of love and respect.

I asked to speak to the sensei when I arrived. I explained to him that I had Cory's heart. At first, he though I meant his spirit and love for others. When I repeated myself and he understood, he had to step away to compose himself.

Bitter or Better; it is your choice

I ask if he wanted me to leave. He replied, "absolutely not, I am deciding how to tell the group." He told me to follow him into the gym. He called the group together and fighting through tears told them, "We talk about how much we miss Cory. This man has his heart."

Everyone immediately had tears in their eyes and lined up to meet me. I knew they needed to hear Cory. I held each person close to my chest as they listened for as long as they wanted. They cried, I cried, Sherry cried, and it was emotionally draining.

There was one comment that most everyone said to me. "Thank you for bringing Cory home! The person that left was not him. Now I know Cory is healthy and helping someone."

Person after person told me how he was an absolute beast when it came to training. He always wanted to train and had a special way to entice someone to join him. The 1979 cult classic, *The Warriors*[2]

This was one of his favorite films. In one scene, while calling out the rival gang, the character clicks soda bottles together and say, “Warriors, come out to play-ee-ay.” He would quote this line to goad the person to come train with him.

I found what I had come for. I had found closure and discovered the background of the person that saved my life. We intended to rest and return home the next day. However, God knew others needed comfort.

One of the members posted on social media that the recipient of Cory heart had dropped by the gym. Cory's aunt responded and asked if I would come by her home the

---

[2] The (Hill, 1979) Warriors, Directed by Walter Hill. New York City. Paramount, 1979

next day. I only thought the previous night had been draining.

I will keep this meeting confidential because it shall remain a private meeting. However, I found out so much about the man. His priority for family, his work ethic, and his absolute commitment to anything he started.

The part of transplant I was not prepared for is the emotional side. I miss Cory and I never met him. I place my hand over my chest every day and tell him I love him. I tell him that his family and friends love him. Most of all they miss him.

I honor Cory every day that I live. Because I know I would not have it without his gift, and more importantly the Grace of God. I ask that each of you to register to be an organ and tissue donor. Be someone's hero, give someone the gift of life.

Bitter or Better; it is your choice

Cory had a tattoo that sums up his personality. I have made it my motto also. *The Fire Inside Me Will Pierce the Darkness.*

Bitter or Better; it is your choice

Beyond

In May 2019 yet another friend went to Heaven before me. I had just talked to James the previous Saturday at our grandson's youth basketball games. I was honored to be asked to speak at my friend's funeral. He was experiencing terrible neck pain and we talked about how debilitating pain was. We both agreed that our Faith and Relationship with Christ held us together. I had asked and received confirmation that he knew Jesus as his Savior.

I have listed the various funerals for several reasons. Death is coming for all of us. Sometimes I wonder why it has not for me. Ron said instead of thinking why, I should realize I have a unique perspective to talk about death. I also was able to comfort the families that I know each person is in Heaven. When I talk to someone, I am going to make sure they know that Jesus is their Savior.

Bitter or Better; it is your choice

In September 2019, the Crabb Family was having a concert at a church in a nearby city. We sat close to the front because I was going to speak to Jason somehow. I had the picture him praying for me pulled up on my phone. I was able to speak and shake hands. I showed him the picture and said, “remember this.”

I told him I was the battery man from NQC the prior year. He stopped, looked at phone, looked at me and I told him, “I got a heart last November.” He now prayed a praise of Praise and Thank You to our Savior.

When I was discharged the nurses, all warned me that hiccups happen, and I would probably be back in a couple of months. I made it 13 months. During my annual they discovered my liver enzymes were elevated. I was given prescription for Repatha. Many people do okay with this drug. My body did not.

Bitter or Better; it is your choice

Everything had been going so well. I was walking a mile each day. I was getting strength enough to work in yard and with my flowers. Now, a nurse is having me get in a wheelchair to be admitted.

More tests were running to find source of pain. It was discovered the biliary duct from liver to gall bladder was inflamed. I had my gall bladder removed in 2005! I discovered the liver still will try and push excess toxin down this duct when it is overloaded. I witnessed to the technician and told my story.

This is encouraged when I volunteered with Legacy of Hope. Have a quick story and tell about the importance of being a Donor. I had been doing this based on my Faith. On the third day, Dr. Pamboukian made rounds. She asked how I felt. I replied, "I feel you need to give this room to someone that needs it." She laughed and agreed. We were on the way home in couple of hours.

However, this made me stop and think. My heart is keeping me alive. At the same time, my body will reject it if I do not take my rejection medicine as I should. Isn't this a picture of Jesus Christ? The very person that gives us eternal life, is rejected if we do not use our anti-rejection meds, Prayer, The Word, and Worship?

I was asked to speak to the Ladies Auxiliary of Cornerstone Presbyterian Church. Ms. Jackie had invited several former co-workers which made me at ease. I spoke and gained an entire new group of prayer warriors. The entire group felt like family. Several from that group are now part of my prayer warrior team.

I keep gaining strength but in November 2020 I was admitted, again. The ECHO revealed that I was at beginning of rejection. Two years post-transplant and I am rejecting. The only issue we could trace for a cause was supplements I had begun taking. They were not FDA approved so they believe was it counter-acted with anti-rejection meds.

I remained in hospital for a week, with five treatments of plasmapheresis. The blood of my body was pumped through a machine which sliced off the top layer of each cell. Laboratory blood was cycled in my body to replace. Afterwards I froze for several hours before my body temperature returned to normal. I had a wonderful talk with technician about Faith.

In December 2020 I am diagnosed with covid. I am given the Monoclonal infusion. I never bounced back like they thought I would. In January 2021 I am admitted. It was the worse three days of loneliness for my entire journey. The nurse had to suit up like my chemotherapy days. Masks, face shield, gown covering and rubber gloves. It felt so sterile. I realized that even checking my pulse felt robotic. Even that human touch would have been a huge deal.

You are in the room with the door closed. There is no walking around or someone popping in to check on you. There were no visitors allowed. The exhaustion on nurse's faces were undeniable. I prayed with each nurse. I prayed with the chaplain that came by each day. This is something I challenge you do to. Ask if you can pray with the people caring for you. Tell them they will be prayed for either way.

The chaplain was the only outside person I could see. Sherry had slept in lobby the night I was admitted. I finally convinced her to go home and rest. The problem was I needed to swap bags with her. This man took my bag to lobby to swap them for me. Just being kind helped me once again.

It has been a year since diagnosed with covid. There are some days I wake up with symptoms, The doctor was very honest when I was discharged. He said we are learning things every day and trying to stay ahead of the spread. Anyone on TV that tells you how covid will react does not know what they are talking about. I think only time will tell for what the virus and vaccination has really done.

I tell people I have several birthdays. Born 1960, accepted Christ 1973, healed from cancer 2005, survived widow maker 2016, the LVAD 2018, and the new heart 2018.

I have been near death six times. I am not actively seeking it. However, one thing has become truly clear. I have realized you will NOT die until it is your time! Coach Bear Bryant once said it is not important how many times you get knocked down. What is important is how many times do you get back up.

I have been plagued with infections since the MRSA staph. I spent the 2018 football national championship game on a heat pad with severe earache. I have had swelling in very uncomfortable places. I will have periods where my joints hurt to simply move. When I was led to write this book, the attacks immediately began. I was diagnosed with Pneumonia and spent most of three weeks in bed or recliner.

I know where the attacks originate. I have prayer warriors that cover me with prayer. I know there is someone standing in the gap for me. I have not made any of this journey without prayer.

I encourage you to seek professional help with the mental stressors. Do not allow yourself to feel that you are all alone. Make sure the counseling is Christian based. My counselor helps me by guiding to scripture. You and I are not the first people in history to need aid.

I try to cherish each day. There is a saying *Yesterday is past, tomorrow is uncertain, but today is a present.*

Bitter or Better; it is your choice

I spend as much time as I can with my grands. When I visit Heather and Bo, we always must go shopping. Bo calls them “Pop Prizes”. At the age of three she already knows that Pop will get her what she wants. I thank God for Liam, Rhett, and Bo. I pour as much into them as I can.

I live each day seeking what God wants me to do. I am still trying to figure out “why am I still here?” I wrote about several funerals on purpose. Each one had an incredible influence on my life. So many have died since my illness started in 2004. There is an underlining guilt in a way. Why was I Healed but they were not?

Think one day it struck me, not one person has ever entered Heaven without being expected. Jesus does not look at someone and tell them they are early. We miss our loved ones so much; we are unable to understand. However, we all have a purpose. When that purpose or calling is fulfilled; God calls us Home.

Bitter or Better; it is your choice

Jesus continues to place people in my path. I hired a man to fix the drainage on our driveway. I mentioned I could not stay out in heat very long because of my health history. When I told him I had been Healed from stage 4B cancer he told me his mother had died with that diagnosis. He said it is good to know that some people make it.

This brings me to the title of this book. One Sunday during my chemo days, the sermon was about how all of us will face trials on earth. The real question was not if, but when.

He continued, "you can either be bitter or better when it occurs. Remember if you get bitter, you will be alone, because who wants to be around a bitter person? Choose to be better, a better friend, a better person, and a better Believer! Then God can use you"

I am reminded of something my dad told me since I was young. "You start to die the moment you are born." We all have an appointed time we will die. Some are young and some are old. We do not decide the time, we do decide if we are ready to see God at the Judgment seat. Please talk to someone if you are not sure your name is written in the Book of Life!

When you read all that has occurred, the thought my go through your head that I just cannot catch a break. With the last years has taught me to Rely on Jesus Christ more than I ever did before.

One thing I never told people is something that happened during my first hospital stay. As I lay in bed, I had a serious discussion about the future possibilities. I ask God to give me any disease or health problem, if it would mean none of my family or friends would ever have to face them.

I have to share one event that 'Only God' brought together. In the Fall of 2019 I went to local natural gas company to check on an account. The woman that helped me had a shirt on for liver disease. God took over from there. I asked who is the shirt for? The reply was "for my grandson, we just found out he has liver disease." (He was 4 months old!)

I place my hands under the cashier window and hear myself saying, "give me your hands, I have been Healed from Stage 4 cancer, prostate cancer, both hips replaced, widow maker heart attack and a heart transplant! The Great Physician will decide your grandson case. Do not let anyone human doctor tell you how this will turn out."

I left knowing only God had placed those words in my mouth. By the time I arrived home she had sent me a note telling me I was a messenger from God. She now had Hope when just that morning she had despair. I was simply obedient in the situation.

<u>Bitter or Better; it is your choice</u>

By the way, the grandmother was a perfect match to be a Living Donor. That little sickly child? He is now a vibrant toddler with a huge future that God has planned for him.

I want to close with a parable that I kept on my desk at work.

One day an old man was walking along the beach which was littered with thousands of starfish. They had been washed ashore by the high tide. He came across a young boy who was eagerly throwing starfish back into the ocean, one by one.

The old man looked at the boy and asked what he was doing. The boy paused, looked up and replied. "Throwing starfish into the ocean. When the sun gets high, they will die; unless I throw them back into the water." The old man scoffed and said, "There are thousands of starfish on this beach. I'm afraid you won't really make much of a difference."

The boy reached down, picked up another starfish and threw it as far as he could into the ocean. Respectfully he turned to the old man, smiled and said, "I made a difference to that one!"

(Eiseley, 1969)

Please, make a difference with the circle around you. You might be the one God has planned to help someone.

I also want to encourage you to become an organ and tissue donor!

SEEKING WHAT COMES NEXT

References

Crabb, G. (1999). Through the Fire [Recorded by C. Family]. KY, USA.

Eiseley, L. (1969). *The Star Thrower.* Retrieved from www.eiseley.org

Hill, W. (Director). (1979). *The Warriors* [Motion Picture].

Made in the USA
Columbia, SC
15 February 2022

56249833R00109